EXTE

SCIENCE

9

Nuclear Power

Selected Topics

R E Lee BSc

Reetchd

Stanley Thornes (Publishers) Ltd

Extending Science Series

1	Air	E N Ramsden and R E Lee
2	Water	E N Ramsden and R E Lee
3	Diseases and Disorders	P T Bunyan
4	Sounds	J J Wellington
5	Metals and Alloys	E N Ramsden
6	Land and Soil	R E Lee
7	Energy	J J Wellington
8	Life Worldwide	T Carrick
9	Nuclear Power	R E Lee
10	Forensic Science	T H James
11	Biotechnology	J Teasdale
12	Pregnancy and Birth	S D Tunnicliffe
13	Sport	R B Arnold

© R E Lee 1986

All rights reserved. No part* of this publication may be reproduced, stored in a retrieval system or transmitted in any form or by any means, electronic, mechanical, photocopying, recording or otherwise, without the prior written consent of the copyright holders. Applications for such permission should be addressed to the publishers: Stanley Thornes (Publishers) Ltd, Old Station Drive, Leckhampton, CHELTENHAM GL53 0DN, UK.

First published in 1986 by
Stanley Thornes (Publishers) Ltd
Old Station Drive
Leckhampton
CHELTENHAM
GL53 0DN

Reprinted 1987

*An exception is made for the word puzzles on pp. 18, 37, 78 and 87. Teachers may photocopy a puzzle to save time for a pupil who would otherwise need to copy from his/her copy of the book. Teachers wishing to make multiple copies of a word puzzle for distribution to a class without individual copies of the book must apply to the publishers in the normal way.

British Library Cataloguing in Publication Data

Lee, R.E.
 Nuclear power.—(Extending science)
 1. Nuclear energy
 I. Title II. Series
 621.48   TK9146
 ISBN 0–85950–554–5

Typeset by Tech-Set, Gateshead, Tyne & Wear
Printed and bound in Great Britain by Ebenezer Baylis & Son Ltd, Worcester.

CONTENTS

Chapter 1 Radiation and its Uses

Where does radioactivity come from?	1	What are the dangers of radiation?	13
What are atoms?	3	What can radiation do to us?	14
What are isotopes?	5	Control of radiation	15
Radioactivity from the nucleus	6	Questions on Chapter 1	16
Uses of radioactivity	6	Crossword on radiation and its uses	18
Half-life of an isotope	12		

Chapter 2 Nuclear Power Stations

Nuclear fission	20	Two-year argument: Sizewell	29
Nuclear reactors	20	No escape from Shoreham	31
Why nuclear power? UKAEA state		Old nuclear power stations	
their case	23	never die	32
Power and potential	24	Fusion ... the answer to our	
Is it safe?	25	energy dreams?	33
Will the environment suffer?	25	Questions on Chapter 2	35
Nuclear accident:		Wordfinder on nuclear power	
Three Mile Island	26	stations	37
The worst nuclear accident:			
Chernobyl, USSR	28		

Chapter 3 Nuclear Waste

What is involved in reprocessing?	38	Village fights waste	48
Disposal of nuclear waste	39	Nuclear dumping at sea ends	49
Sellafield: the nuclear laundry	44	Transport of nuclear waste on land	49
Nuclear cocktail?	47	Questions on Chapter 3	52
Bugs in the nuclear bin?	48		

Chapter 4 Bombs and Missiles

How nuclear bombs work	53	Missiles	64
The bomb connection	55	Women for Peace	69
Atomic destruction	56	Campaign for Nuclear Disarmament	70
When the bomb drops	59	Star Wars	74
Broken arrow	60	Questions on Chapter 4	77
Nuclear tests	62	Crossword on bombs and missiles	78

Chapter 5   **Nuclear War**

Are we prepared for a nuclear
   attack?   79
World War Three   82
Who's afraid of the cold and dark?   83

Chances of survival in the UK   84
Prevention is better than cure   84
Questions on Chapter 5   86
Wordfinder on nuclear war   87

Solutions to crosswords and
   wordfinders   88

Index   89

PREFACE

I have written this book because I am interested in nuclear power. I care deeply about the environment and hope to generate some enthusiasm for its preservation in this book. I think that all of us should understand nuclear power, its great value and its dangers. Uranium and plutonium are the answers to our prayers for energy, but they must be used responsibly.

I offer this book to teachers to use in any manner that suits them and their pupils. It may be used as extension material for a physics or chemistry course. It may be used for social sciences, general studies or environmental science. I hope too that older pupils who find a traditional course too academic for their liking may find some interesting reading here.

Robert E Lee
St. George's College, Weybridge

ACKNOWLEDGEMENTS

I would like to thank my 'nuclear family', wife Elizabeth and young son Jonathan, for their encouragement during the writing of this book.

Janet Stone of the picture library, UKAEA, was particularly helpful with choice of photographs and I am most grateful. The author and publishers are grateful to the following: United Kingdom Energy Authority for the cover photographs and those in pages 2, 4, 7, 8, 10–12, 21–24, 34, 35, 42, 44, 45 and 48, and for the table on page 15; Central Electricity Generating Board for the photographs on pages 30, 50 and 51; Ministry of Defence for the letter on page 72; Campaign for Nuclear Disarmament for the letter on page 73; Dr S Openshaw, Newcastle University, for the illustration on page 60.

RADIATION AND ITS USES

WHERE DOES RADIOACTIVITY COME FROM?

Nothing at all was known about radioactivity until 1896. This was the year when a French scientist, Antoine Becquerel, discovered radiation by mistake. It was probably the most important development in modern physics. Becquerel had been studying some uranium compounds. He had wrapped a uranium compound in paper and left it by accident near a photographic plate. The uranium had given off (emitted) something which left marks on the plate, when it was developed. The uranium was radiating something like X-rays.

Radiation affects many aspects of our lives

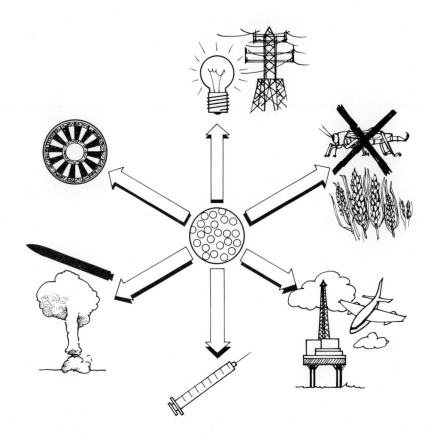

1

An English scientist, Ernest Rutherford, studied the nature of these radiations further. He found that there were two distinct kinds of radiation being given off. One kind he called alpha-radiation. Alpha-radiation can be stopped by a thin sheet of paper. The other kind he called beta-radiation and it can pass through paper but can be stopped by a thin sheet of metal foil.

Another French scientist, Pierre Villard, discovered that there was a third kind of radiation. This could pass through both paper and thin metal foils. It was stopped by concrete. This was called gamma-radiation, to complete the first three letters of the Greek alphabet, alpha, beta, gamma.

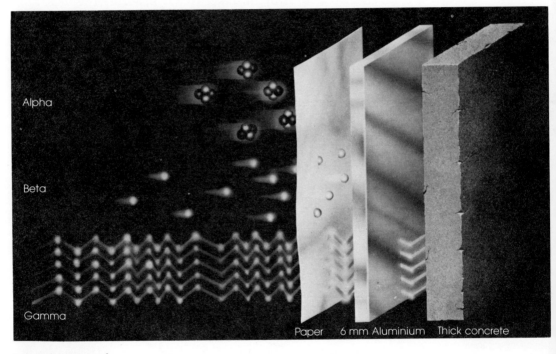

Alpha

Beta

Gamma

Paper   6 mm Aluminium   Thick concrete

Penetrating power of
alpha, beta and
gamma radiation

Radiation	Symbol	Penetrating power
Alpha	α-	Cannot go through paper or skin
Beta	β-	Can go through skin but is stopped by thin metal foils
Gamma	γ-	Can go through skin and thin metal foils Stopped by concrete or lead

Scientists were beginning to think that radiation was only connected with uranium. Soon they found that other elements such as potassium, rubidium and thorium also emitted radiation.

Marie Curie, a Polish scientist living in France, worked on pitchblende. This was a natural rock containing uranium. It puzzled Madame Curie that pitchblende emitted four times the radiation that a pure uranium compound did. Did it contain some hidden ingredient more active than uranium? She worked on separating the pitchblende in a furnace. It was not easy, and took her over a year. By 1898 she had found the hidden ingredients. Two new elements, polonium and radium, had been discovered in the pitchblende. These new elements emitted much stronger radiation than uranium. The radium emitted several million times the radiation expected from uranium. Sadly, Madame Curie had not realised that this radiation was extremely harmful. It caused the blood cancer, leukaemia, and she died.

Any element that gives off radiation is said to be *radioactive*. To understand where the radiation is coming from we need to know something about *atoms*.

WHAT ARE ATOMS?

It is not easy to describe atoms because we cannot see them. But we can see the effect when a large number of them are grouped together. People, buildings and objects such as school desks are examples of millions of atoms grouped together. Air is invisible but it contains atoms; they are so far apart they cannot be seen. (The space between the atoms in air contains nothing at all. This 'nothing' is known as a *vacuum*.)

Atoms contain three types of smaller particle within them. Two of these particles have an electrical charge and the third has no charge at all.

Particle in an atom	Charge	Mass
Electron	Negative	Hardly any mass
Proton	Positive	About 2000 times that of the electron
Neutron	None	Same as the proton

There are lots of different atoms but they are always made up from the three types of particles. They only differ in the *number* of each type of particle present in the atom.

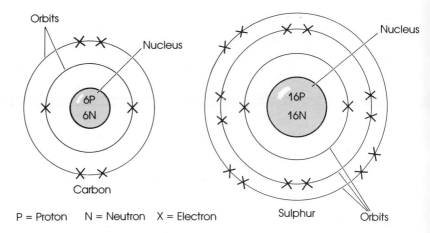

Atoms of the elements carbon and sulphur

Orbits
Nucleus

6P
6N

Carbon

Nucleus

16P
16N

Sulphur

Orbits

P = Proton   N = Neutron   X = Electron

By observing the illustrations of carbon and sulphur atoms, a pattern should emerge. The protons and neutrons are always in the middle of the atom. This middle is called the *nucleus*. The electrons *orbit* (go round) the nucleus much as the planets orbit the Sun. You should also see a number pattern: the number of protons in any atom equals the number of electrons. The number of neutrons does not follow such a regular pattern.

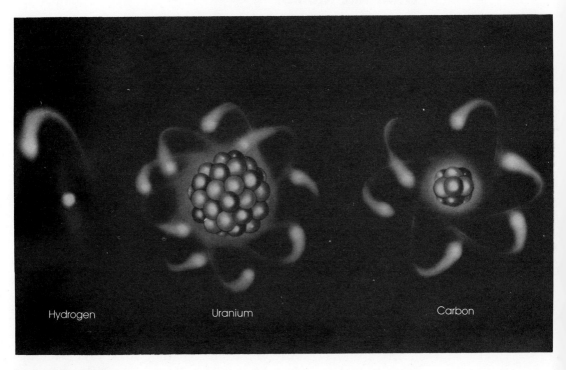

Hydrogen   Uranium   Carbon

Some atoms showing
a 3-dimensional look

Atomic particle	Where in the atom?	Number in the atom
Electron	Orbiting the nucleus	Same as number of protons
Proton	In the nucleus	Same as number of electrons
Neutrons	In the nucleus	No particular pattern

WHAT ARE ISOTOPES?

You will remember that we said that there is no particular pattern to the number of neutrons in an atom. If two atoms vary *only* in their number of neutrons, they are said to be *isotopes* of one another. They will have different masses because one has more neutrons than the other. The sum of the neutrons and protons in an atom is called the *mass number*.

Isotopes of uranium

Number of				
Protons	Neutrons	Electrons	Mass Number	Known as
92	143	92	235	Uranium-235
92	146	92	238	Uranium-238

Isotopes of chlorine

Number of				
Protons	Neutrons	Electrons	Mass Number	Known as
17	18	17	35	Chlorine-35
17	20	17	37	Chlorine-37

Isotopes

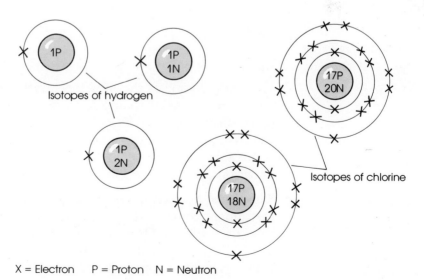

Isotopes of hydrogen

Isotopes of chlorine

X = Electron   P = Proton   N = Neutron

5

RADIOACTIVITY FROM THE NUCLEUS

Many atoms do not give out radiation. If they *do not* give out radiation they are said to be *non-radioactive isotopes*. The ones that *do* give out radiation are called *radioactive isotopes*.

Why do some atoms give out radiation while others do not? It seems to depend on the number of neutrons compared to the number of protons in the nucleus. If there are too many, or too few, neutrons then the nucleus is *unstable*. The unstable nucleus tries to become more stable by giving out some particles as radiation. The radiation comes from the centre of the atom, the nucleus. The particles of radiation are given off with considerable force (energy) as shown by their ability to penetrate objects. Gamma radiation is more like waves of energy rather than particles. These are very much like X-rays.

USES OF RADIOACTIVITY

Radioactive isotopes have many uses. They are used in nuclear power stations, nuclear weapons, medicine, agriculture and engineering. They have been used to find the age of the Dead Sea Scrolls and King Arthur's Table. Some heart pacemakers gain their energy from a radioactive isotope. Isotopes also supply the energy to send signals from satellites to earth. The path taken by dangerous pollution can be traced by including radioactive isotopes in the pollution. This last example involves the isotope as a *tracer*. The tracer isotope gives out radiation which can be detected using a Geiger counter. Wherever the tracer goes, the counter picks it up.

Medical uses

Radiation therapy

Gamma-radiation is the most penetrating of all the forms of radiation. It is used to attack cancer cells (cells growing out of control). Fortunately, radiation attacks cancer cells more effectively than it attacks normal cells. However, if great care is not taken all cells are destroyed. For maximum effect the radiation must hit the cancer target only.

The Royal Free Hospital in London has a radiation therapy instrument controlled by computer. The computer makes sure that the radiation hits the target. The gamma-radiation is supplied by the cobalt-60 isotope. This instrument destroys many types of cancer including tumours.

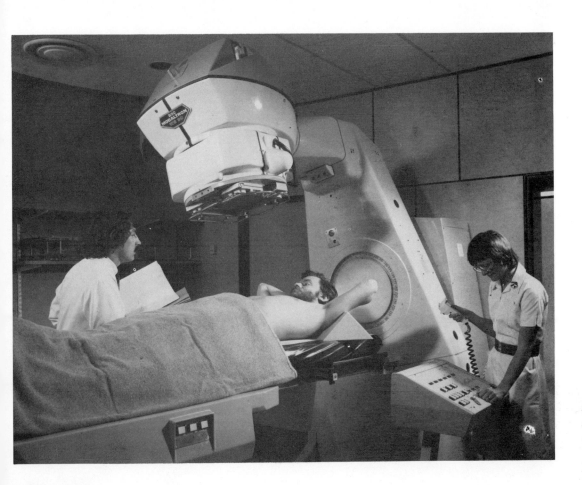

Radiation therapy
controlled by computer

Kidney efficiency

If a patient has kidney trouble it may affect one or both
kidneys. Often one kidney will be working quite well. A
radioactive tracer can be used to find out which kidney is
inefficient. The tracer is injected into the patient's blood-
stream. A Geiger counter measures the amount of radiation
coming from each kidney. If the kidney is normal, the radioactivity should rise for four minutes then drop sharply. If it is
not working properly, the radiation will not rise or fall so
quickly.

There are other examples of the use of radioactive tracers in
medicine, e.g. checking on our thyroid glands (which help to
control our growth) to make sure they are getting necessary
iodine. An iodine isotope tracer is used.

Sterilising medical supplies

When a patient has an operation, it is essential that no germs enter the wound. This is why instruments have to be sterilised before they are germ-free.

Medical instruments may be sterilised in boiling water or by using chemicals. Neither of these methods is completely successful. Radiation destroys germs and so it is used to sterilise medical supplies. It is passed through the sealed bags containing the dressings and instruments. They are then ready for use at any time. Often the instruments are only used once and then thrown away. Radiation is an easy and effective way to sterilise medical supplies.

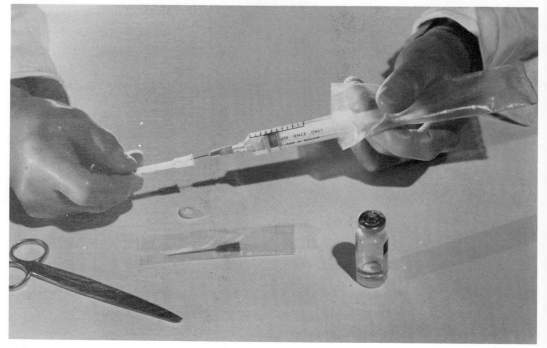

Fitting together disposable needle and syringe after gamma sterilisation

Agricultural uses

High yield crops

If mild radiation is passed through seeds many of them change. Some change for the better and some for the worse. After radiation the seeds are tested and only the successful ones (the most hardy) are used by the farmer. There are many cases of corn or wheat being improved in this way.

In Japan, a favourite type of rice plant was found to flatten in heavy rains or wind. Radiation was passed through the rice seeds. Some seeds changed for the better because of this.

They grew into plants which could stand up in high wind and rain. By collecting and planting seeds from these strong plants, more strong plants were produced. Now the rice crop is successful.

Radiation passed through seeds can even make some resistant to disease when they grow into plants.

Fertiliser efficiency

A farmer wishes to use the best, most efficient, fertiliser that he can find. A radioactive tracer can be used to see how good the fertiliser is. It can measure *how quickly* fertiliser gets into a plant. Also it can show *how much* fertiliser gets into the plant.

To compare phosphate fertilisers, a radioactive phosphorus isotope is used. If it gets into the plant quickly the Geiger counter will show this. If a lot of the isotope gets into the plant the counter will give a high reading. The most efficient fertiliser gets into the plant quickly and in the greatest amount.

Insect control

If a mild radiation is passed into insects, it can destroy their power to reproduce. Many insects are pests because they destroy enormous quantities of crops. Radiation is just one of many ways to reduce this crop loss.

In the case of the Mediterranean fruit fly, radiation proved quite successful. Great numbers of the male flies were reared artificially. They were then treated with radiation from a cobalt source. This stopped their powers to mate successfully. They were released into the wild and mated but produced no offspring. This kept the numbers down and thus saved crops.

Radioactive insecticides are sometimes applied to the leaves of plants to study how effective they are. Insects on the leaves are tested with a Geiger counter. A good insecticide will be one which is shown by the counter to have been taken in large amounts by the insects.

Engineering uses

Metal fatigue

When metals are subjected to forces such as stretching and twisting over long periods of time, they change. There is nothing to see, but the metal becomes very weak. This is called metal fatigue. It is a very dangerous situation if it is not spotted in time.

Aircraft wings, for example, have to be checked very carefully for metal fatigue. Gamma-radiation can be used to spot the weakness (X-rays are not strong enough). Radiation is passed through the wing and a photograph collected on the other side. Little hairline cracks due to metal fatigue are then visible.

Radioisotope inspection on a British Airways Boeing 747

Thickness gauge

If a known amount of radiation is passed into a material, its thickness can be found by measuring the radiation on the other side. This is the way that they make sure that sheets of plastic and aluminium are produced with the same thickness; as long as the collected radiation is the same, then the thickness is the same.

The wall thickness of a pipe carrying a liquid can be found by a similar method. A radioactive isotope is introduced into the liquid flow. A Geiger counter outside the tube measures the radiation. If the wall of the pipe is thick, the radiation coming out will be small. The size of the counter reading can give a value for the thickness of the pipe wall.

Leaks in long underground pipes have been found by using radiation. A radioactive isotope is included in the liquid, which could be oil, for example. At the site of the leak, a Geiger counter on the surface above will show a high reading even though the leak is underground. This can save a lot of time and money trying to locate a leak.

Plastics and rubber

When plastics are made their properties depend on how well the groups of atoms stick together. If radiation is passed through the plastic these groups immediately stick together much better. Different types of building materials bond together well when radiation is passed through them.

When rubber is hardened it is said to be *vulcanised*. This used to be done by adding sulphur to the rubber. If radiation is passed through the rubber it vulcanises it. Tyres for cars are often hardened in this way.

Oil platform safety

The safety of oil rigs in the North Sea can be checked by radioactivity. A tracer is added to the concrete used to attach the rig's legs to the sea bed. The North Sea is very rough and can cause the concrete to move, making the platform unsafe. By monitoring the radioactivity from within the rig's legs, it can be seen whether the foundations are moving.

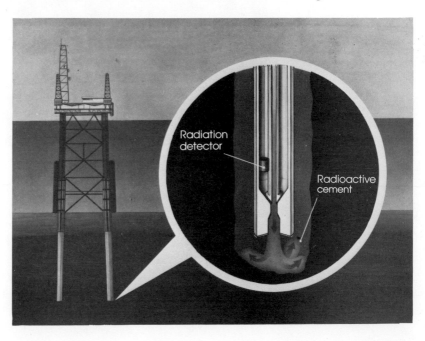

Thistle Oil Rig with radioactive cement

Radiation detector

Radioactive cement

Radioactive dating

King Arthur's Table

Some radioactive isotopes occur naturally. One such isotope is carbon-14. It occurs in all living tissue and things made from plant and animal material, such as wood and paper. The amount of radiation given out by wood or paper depends on its age. The older the wood or paper, the less the radiation.

Scientists at Harwell were asked to find the age of King Arthur's Table. The table is on show at the Great Hall, Castle Yard, in Winchester. The legendary King Arthur is said to have used it in the 5th century AD but scientists found that the table dated from the 13th century AD.

King Arthur's Table, Great Hall, Castle Yard, Winchester

HALF-LIFE OF AN ISOTOPE

Do radioactive isotopes give out radiation forever? The simple answer is no, but some do go on for a long time. When such an isotope drops its radiation level by half, the time taken is called the *half-life*. This new level of radiation then drops by one half during the next half-life.

Half-life illustration

Half-life

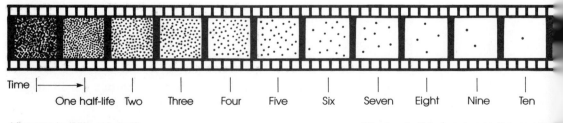

Time

One half-life Two Three Four Five Six Seven Eight Nine Ten

After one half-life only half the radioactivity remains

After ten half-lives only one-thousandth of the radioactivity remains

12

The illustration shows that after ten such half-lives just one-thousandth of the original radiation exists. The half-life is a fixed value for a particular isotope. It gives us some idea of how long the radioactivity will last. Note that it will last much longer than two half-lives!

Isotope	Half-life
Carbon-14	5 570 years
Sodium-24	15 hours
Cobalt-60	5 years
Iodine-131	8 days
Plutonium-242	379 000 years

You will see that half-lives vary a great deal. If the type of radiation is strong and the half-life is long, the radiation is not going to go away. This is true of plutonium-242, which is being pumped into the sea as nuclear waste. It will be giving off dangerous radiation for many generations to come.

Quite the opposite is true of iodine-131, which can be used as a medical tracer in the body. There is little danger because the half-life is short and so it will not radiate for long.

WHAT ARE THE DANGERS OF RADIATION?

We should first consider the various ways that radiation reaches us. Most of the radiation we receive comes from the air. This radiation is entirely natural and not due to any human activity. The materials used in buildings give off some radioactivity and there is radiation from the ground too. These two, buildings and ground, make up a large part of the radiation in our environment. Our food and drink is also radioactive. Cosmic rays are rays from outer-space and these also contribute to the level of radiation in the atmosphere. Every time you have an X-ray or doctors give you a radio-active isotope for tracing illness, you receive some radiation. Not enough to make you want to stop the treatment though!

You will see that the contribution made by nuclear weapons testing and nuclear power is very small overall. However, it is more concentrated in some areas, around nuclear power stations for example. There is also some very small radiation involved in air travel. This is because the aircraft is closer to radiation caused by rays from outer space.

It is true that much of the radiation cannot be avoided.

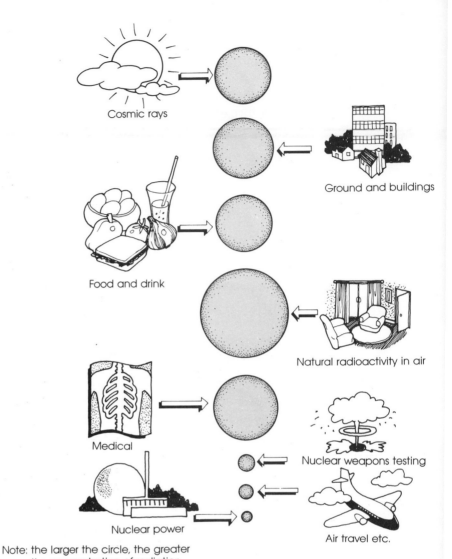

Sources of radiation

Cosmic rays

Ground and buildings

Food and drink

Natural radioactivity in air

Medical

Nuclear weapons testing

Nuclear power

Air travel etc.

Note: the larger the circle, the greater the concentration of radiation

WHAT CAN RADIATION DO TO US?

The cells in our body can be affected by radiation. When we grow, cells have to divide into new cells. Radiation can stop this proper growth. Other things that cells should do in our bodies may also be stopped, because of radiation. For example, it may no longer be possible to reproduce and thus have babies. Radiation has resulted in a worrying effect in some animals. They have produced deformed offspring. When defects are passed on to the next generation in this way they are said to be *hereditary*.

Some cancers have been shown to be due to radiation. Large doses of radiation do widespread damage to the gut, to blood cells and to bone tissues. Doses like this generally lead to death within a few weeks. Early effects of such a dose are skin burns and loss of hair.

Smaller doses of radiation, or doses spread out over a period of time, do not produce the early effects. There is a slight risk of getting cancer and hereditary effects seem to be limited to animals.

We have talked of the various ways radiation gets to us. The doses of radiation we get from day to day cannot be linked to any illnesses. This does not mean that such doses are absolutely harmless. The risks of illness from this radiation are very small indeed.

The risk chart shows that there is much more chance of us dying because of the flu or a road accident than dying from radiation:

	Annual risk of death
Heart disease	1 in 300
Cancer	1 in 400
Flu	1 in 4000
Road accidents	1 in 7000
Lightning	1 in 6 million
Usual radiation	1 in 60 000
Radiation from the nuclear industry *alone*	1 in 30 million.

CONTROL OF RADIATION

The amount of radiation received by anybody working with radiation is closely controlled. They wear film-badges which are regularly checked. The badges show how much radiation has been received during the period. If it is too much, that person must be rested from radiation work. There is a maximum dose of radiation that such workers can take in a year. Nurses working with X-rays also observe this procedure. X-rays were often used to check the condition of a baby in its mother's womb in the past. These days such X-rays are kept to a minimum to prevent any damage to the baby.

The United Kingdom Government has strict controls over the radiation released into the air or sea by nuclear industries. Possible sources of radiation are surrounded by thick layers of lead and concrete which absorb the radiation because of their high *density*. This leads to more safety. Nuclear power stations are built to withstand any type of accident. It is said that they would survive earthquakes or plane crashes without leaking radiation.

If radiation is released into water or air there will always be some danger to humans. There are various routes that could send the radiation back to us. These routes are called *pathways*. Some pathways are more dangerous than others and these are called *critical pathways*.

Radiation released to the air could go straight into our lungs. Alternatively, the pathway could be

$$plant \rightarrow animal \rightarrow meat \rightarrow human$$

Other possible routes are

$$plant \rightarrow cow \rightarrow milk \rightarrow human$$
$$plant \rightarrow human$$

Similarly, with radiation released to water. Alternatives are

$$water \rightarrow human$$

or

$$water \rightarrow aquatic \ plant \rightarrow fish \rightarrow human$$

Radiation in the air and water is regularly monitored. Regular samples of fish and milk are also taken to check for radiation. This assures that levels are not creeping up and presenting a danger.

QUESTIONS ON CHAPTER 1

In questions 1–5, supply words to fill in the blanks. Do not write on this page.

1 The French scientists _____ and _____ both contributed to the discovery of radiation. _____ was the first to observe radiation and _____ discovered the most penetrating radiation known as _____ radiation.

2 Madame _____ worked on a substance called _____ . She was amazed that it was _____ times as radioactive as _____ . Tragically she died of _____ . She did discover two new elements, _____ and _____ .

3 An atom is a very small thing and contains _____ and _____ in the middle part, known as the _____ . _____ orbit the middle part of the atom. There are always equal numbers of _____ and _____ in an atom. The number of _____ does not follow any particular _____ .

4 Isotopes of an element have the same number of ____ and ____ but differ in the number of ____ . The one with the most ____ is the heaviest one. Some isotopes are radioactive and therefore give off ____ .

5 There are ____ types of radiation, ____ , beta, and ____ . The ____ radiation is ____ X-rays, and is the most ____ and only stopped by ____ or ____ .

6 Fill in the missing numbers in the following table of isotopes

Protons	Neutrons	Electrons	Mass number	Known as
*	6	6	12	Carbon-12
13	*	13	27	Aluminium-27
47	60	*	107	Silver-107
50	70	50	*	Tin-120
1	2	1	3	Hydrogen-*

7 Why are some atoms radioactive and others not?

8 What is a radioactive tracer?
Describe a use for such a tracer in (a) medicine, (b) agriculture and (c) engineering.

9 What are the good effects of passing radiation through seeds?

10 Compare old methods of sterilising medical supplies with the latest method.

11 What is the purpose of passing radiation through some insects?

12 What is metal fatigue? How can it be detected?

13 Tell the King Arthur's Table story in your own words. Why is it disappointing?

14 List the different ways that radiation gets to us. Is the radiation from nuclear power and weapons testing important?

15 What is meant by hereditary effects of radiation?

16 Compare the chances of dying from (a) the flu and (b) lightning, with the chances from the nuclear radiation industry alone.

17 What does a large dose of radiation do to us?

18 How can we minimise the amount of radiation that we receive?

19 What regular radiation tests are done to protect us?

CROSSWORD ON RADIATION AND ITS USES

First, trace this grid on to a piece of paper (or photocopy this page — teacher, please see the note at the front of the book). Then fill in the answers. Do not write on this page.

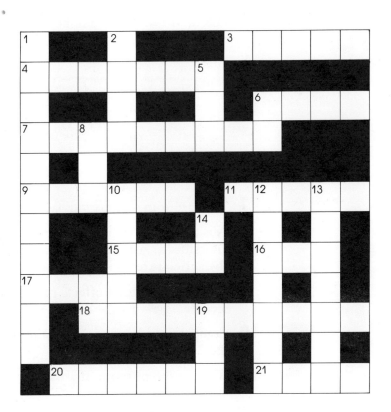

Across

3 _____ can attack when human resistance is lowered by radiation (5)

4 An _____ is the same element but different mass (7)

6 Radiation stopped by thin metal foils (4)

7 Subject involving the study of elements and their compounds (9)

9 Film-_____ are used to detect exposure to radiation (6)

11 French scientist who died studying radiation (5)

15 Liquid tested to show radiation through the food chain (4)

16 Radiation is an _____ to dating and tracing (3)

17 The usual level of radiation (4)

18 Particles or waves given out from the nucleus (10)

20 King _____ did not use the table (6)

21 The _____ number is equal to the number of protons plus neutrons (4)

Down

1 Radioactive substance that yielded two new elements (11)
2 It has a nucleus orbited by electrons (4)
5 To _____ is one way to gain radiation (3)
8 A full dose of radiation could spell the _____ (3)
10 The most damaging radiation (5)
12 They once thought this was the only radioactive element (7)
13 _____'s isotope is a good medical tracer (7)
14 United Kingdom (2)
19 This must be regularly sampled for radiation (3)

CHAPTER 2

NUCLEAR POWER STATIONS

NUCLEAR FISSION

Certain very heavy isotopes such as uranium mass number 235 and plutonium-239, break up when a neutron hits them. The nucleus breaks into roughly equal parts and this is known as *fission*. Enormous amounts of energy are released during fission and two or three neutrons. Each neutron hits another isotope. This process, once started, 'feeds' itself and soon gets out of control. It is known as a *chain reaction*. The chain reaction takes place very quickly and so, before long, millions of atoms have broken and their released neutrons are about to break other atoms. Harmful radiation is given off at the same time. It is this radiation that gives rise to the great fears about nuclear power.

The great attraction of this kind of chain reaction is the vast amount of heat energy given off from a small mass of starting material. One gram of uranium-235 will produce the same amount of heat energy as 2000 kilograms of coal. What a useful fuel we have in uranium, and the same can be said of plutonium. They are the basis of nuclear power. They are also the basis for nuclear bombs. Uranium-235 has been nicknamed *honey venom* because of its great potential as a fuel, and its great danger to life.

NUCLEAR REACTORS

A nuclear reactor is just like an oil-fired or coal-fired power station, but the fuel is uranium or plutonium. In each, the heat generated converts water into steam. This steam drives a turbine which produces electricity.

Neutron → Uranium-235 → Forms unstable atom
→ Splits in two → Releases great energy plus two or three neutrons. These neutrons do the same to other uranium-235 atoms

The uranium-235 chain reaction. Atoms break as they release neutrons . . . fission

n = Neutron

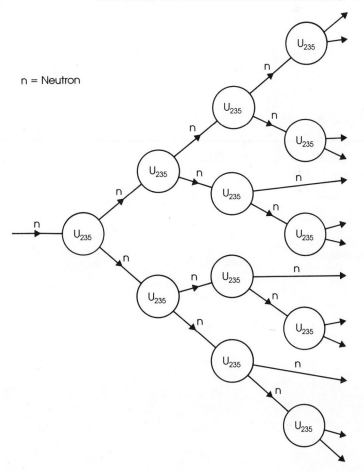

All types of nuclear reactor use uranium-235 or plutonium-239 as a fuel. A *moderator,* such as graphite, is used to slow down the neutrons. This controls the speed of the reaction so as to give the maximum energy from the fuel rods. A *coolant* is used to take away the heat produced by the fission process. The coolant may be liquid sodium, water, or a gas. In some reactors the coolant also performs the moderating task.

The nuclear power programme in the UK started in 1956 with a Magnox station (see table below) at Calder Hall in Cumberland. It was the world's first large-scale nuclear power station. Other types of nuclear reactors have been developed since. These vary in their fuel-type, coolant and moderator. The most common types of reactor are shown in the table below.

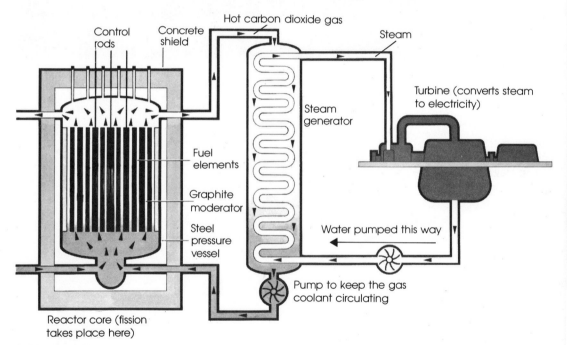

Basic gas-cooled reactor (Magnox)

Name of reactor	Fuel	Coolant	Moderator
Magnox (named after a mixture of magnesium and other metals surrounding fuel)	Uranium-235 rods	Carbon dioxide	Graphite
AGR (Advanced gas-cooled reactor)	Uranium oxide	Carbon dioxide	Graphite
PWR (Pressurised water reactor)	Uranium oxide	Water	Water
Fast reactor	Uranium and plutonium oxides	Liquid sodium	None

The UK's first nuclear power station, Calder Hall

The fast reactor deserves a special mention. It is called 'fast' because it has no moderator to slow down the neutrons. The fast neutrons help the reactor to produce heat more quickly. Liquid sodium takes this heat away equally quickly to produce electricity. Fast reactors may be used to produce their own additional supplies of fuel. This can be done by surrounding the plutonium core with a *blanket* of uranium-238. The useless uranium-238 is converted to plutonium-239 fuel. Such a reactor is known as a *breeder*, because it makes its own fuel. There is a Prototype Fast Reactor (PFR) at Dounreay, Scotland. This has been operating successfully for over ten years. Information gained from its performance will help in the design of commercial fast reactors in the future.

WHY NUCLEAR POWER?

Many say that supplies of oil and gas are running out in the long term. Even if we are careful not to waste energy we may still need nuclear power. The UK has large coal reserves but much of these should be used to make chemicals when the oil runs out. Plastics, fertilisers and substitute oils can be made from coal. There is a limit to the contributions that wind, wave and solar power can make; some experts think that such power would give only 4% of our energy requirements if big efforts were made.

Nuclear energy is not new. It has been making electricity safely for thirty years in the UK. It is a relatively cheap form of energy.

The Dounreay fast reactor

POWER AND POTENTIAL

About one-sixth of the UK's electricity is at present produced by nuclear energy. Uranium, unlike coal, has no other commercial uses. One ton of uranium can produce the same amount of electricity as 25 000 tonnes of coal. With the fast reactors planned, one tonne of uranium will replace one and a half million tonnes of coal. Using these fast reactors we seem to have enough uranium for 250 years. Coal reserves would last about the same time if used instead of uranium.

The newest nuclear power stations give cheaper electricity than the latest coal-fired stations. The CEGB estimate that they can save consumers £1000 million by building a *pressurised water reactor*, PWR, power station at Sizewell. The United States, Japan, France, the USSR and West Germany all have more nuclear power than us.

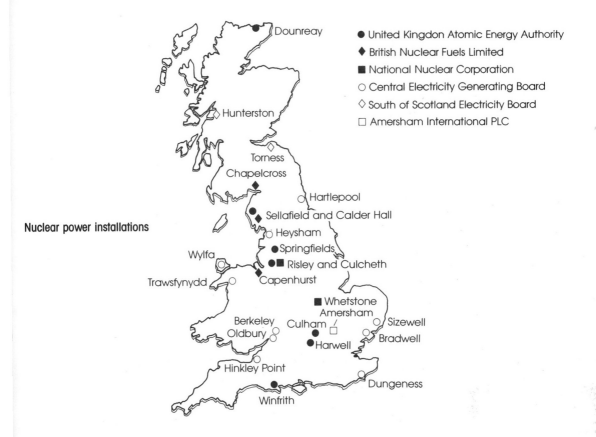

Nuclear power installations

Dounreay

● United Kingdon Atomic Energy Authority
♦ British Nuclear Fuels Limited
■ National Nuclear Corporation
○ Central Electricity Generating Board
◇ South of Scotland Electricity Board
□ Amersham International PLC

Hunterston

Torness
Chapelcross
Hartlepool
Sellafield and Calder Hall
Heysham
Wylfa
Springfields
Risley and Culcheth
Trawsfynydd
Capenhurst
Whetstone
Amersham
Berkeley
Culham
Sizewell
Oldbury
Bradwell
Harwell
Hinkley Point
Dungeness
Winfrith

IS IT SAFE?

The Health and Safety Executive is the Government department whose job it is to ensure that we are protected against danger. It claims that nuclear power is as safe as burning oil or coal for electricity. Nuclear power stations are designed and built for safety. They also claim there has not been a single radiation accident injuring a member of the public in 30 years of operation. A nuclear power station cannot explode like a bomb because the uranium is not concentrated enough.

The transportation of spent nuclear fuel is safe. Not one container has been broken open during four million miles of rail journeys.

Radiation is a natural phenomenon and was not invented by the nuclear industry. Most of our radiation comes from natural sources.

WILL THE ENVIRONMENT SUFFER?

A nuclear power station covers an area of about 10 hectares. Windmills would have to cover 20 235 hectares to give the same amount of electricity. The wastes can be stored in glass.

Plutonium is a product of modern reactors. This can be used as fuel in a fast reactor where it is burnt up. Plutonium is a hazardous material but not the most poisonous known. Few poisons are as safely guarded as plutonium. So nuclear power takes up little area, waste can be stored safely and the poisons contained. The UKAEA feel that on this basis the environment is not threatened.

NUCLEAR ACCIDENT: Three Mile Island

When the *pressurised water reactor,* PWR, nuclear power station was built at Three Mile Island the chances of an accident were quoted as being near zero. The site at Harrisburg in the State of Pennsylvania, USA contained two reactor units. They had multiple safety systems, the best engineering design and experienced operators.

Things started to go wrong at 4 am on 28 March 1979. Four operators were on duty in Unit Two when a faulty valve on top of the pressurising vessel failed to close. The advanced computer assumed that the valve had closed and then gave false information. The computer printout was one and a half hours behind events.

A gauge indicated that the pressure vessel was filling with water; in fact water was rushing out. Operators assumed that the gauge was right and closed two valves. As a result the reactor core was starved of cooling water. The reactor core got hotter and hotter and the operators realised that the gauge had misled them. They switched on the emergency core cooling system. This sent thousands of litres of water directly through the core. Unfortunately the core had already melted some zirconium metal surrounding it. This molten metal reacted with the water to make explosive hydrogen gas. The hydrogen exploded in the pressure vessel.

Over $3\frac{1}{2}$ million litres of water were radioactive from the core. Radiation was released to the atmosphere from the water. The reactor core got too hot and melted. The early stages of melt-down had been reached. Fortunately, the molten core did not burn into the earth below.

The reactor was crippled. Four giant cooling towers were out of action because the water was dangerously radioactive. The building next to the reactor core contained the millions of litres of radioactive water.

What lessons can be drawn from this experience? The claim that the safety system could cope with the multiple failures was obviously not true. This reactor could only deal with 'single failure' accidents. Also many of the operators were found to be poorly trained. They were unqualified for the demanding tasks in a power station. They seemed only qualified to run the station when things were going well. There is a big difference between the ideal reactor and the real world one!

Nuclear melt-down

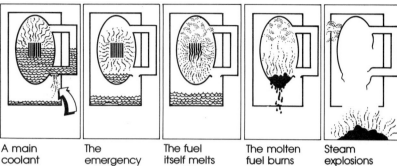

A main coolant pipe ruptures and the core temperature rises

The emergency cooling system also fails and the fuel rods melt

The fuel itself melts and the core fills with hot radioactive gases.

The molten fuel burns through the pressure vessel and containment dome

Steam explosions fling metal parts through the dome walls ... while the molten uranium burns down into the earth

The owners of the nuclear power station could not afford to decontaminate the site after the accident. The Governor and his staff in Harrisburg reluctantly agreed to help with the cost of the clean up. They only helped because they felt the site might become a monument to the failure of the nuclear power industry.

Following this accident, many Americans showed in a poll that they had lost confidence in nuclear power. There were no new orders for these reactors during the two years after the accident. The industry faced melt-down itself.

The owners of the site, Metropolitan Edison, could claim that not one person died in this accident. The steel-lined concrete pressure vessels, several metres thick, worked as safety barriers and protected the people.

The arguments still continue. On 30 May 1985 the row over re-opening the plant came to a head. The Nuclear Regulatory Commission gave permission to reopen the plant. The State Governor and Senators of Pennsylvania opposed the opening. They applied to the courts for an injunction to prevent work starting on 11 June. Hundreds of demonstrators blocked the gates to the Three Mile Island site shouting 'killers' and 'murderers'. It is significant that this feeling of outrage exists six full years after the accident. To this day, work has still been prevented.

THE WORST NUCLEAR ACCIDENT: Chernobyl, USSR

On 25 April 1986, an accident occurred in one of the four reactors at the Chernobyl nuclear power station near Kiev in Russia. It was an RBMK 1000 megawatt reactor, fuelled by uranium, moderated by graphite and cooled by pressurised water. The full facts are not yet known. We do know that the reactor core began to overheat (probably because the cooling water had been lost). Steam reacted with the graphite to produce hydrogen, which caused an explosion, followed by a fire. The explosion blew off the roof of the reactor and sent a cloud of radioactive fall-out into the atmosphere.

On 28 April, Sweden, unaware of a nuclear accident in Russia, reported increased levels of radiation in the atmosphere. It had been carried on the wind from Chernobyl. As the wind direction changed, other European countries noticed an increase in radiation levels. The Russians, in response to the Swedish discovery, issued a brief statement admitting the accident. One week later, the UK measured fall-out in its atmosphere for the first time. In the area around Kiev, the air, soil, water and, consequently, the food were contaminated. People were evacuated from the area of the accident, but some have died and many more are suffering from radiation sickness.

Western experts have called this the world's worst nuclear accident. At the time of writing it is still too early to say what the long-term effects will be. Cancer caused by exposure to radiation will take years to appear. The Chernobyl incident has caused general concern about the safety of the nuclear power industry and its future.

Chernobyl: its position in relation to the rest of Europe

TWO YEAR ARGUMENT: Sizewell

The Central Electricity Generating Board, CEGB, want to install a nuclear power station at Sizewell in Suffolk. They already have a nuclear power station there of the Magnox type. The new one would be known as Sizewell B power station. Public inquiries are usually organised to give everyone a chance to argue for or against proposed power stations. In the early days of nuclear power, inquiries only took a few days. The Sizewell B inquiry has taken two years. Why such a fuss over a second power station on the site? The type of power station is new to the UK and there is distrust about its safety. It is a PWR, common in the United States of America.

How can people discuss a power station for two years? There are many experts to consult, and they often disagree. There are many pressure groups such as Friends of the Earth, FOE, and the Campaign for Nuclear Disarmament, CND, and they must all have their say. This inquiry is very important. It will decide the pattern of nuclear power in the UK well into the next century.

The first year of the inquiry dealt with the need for Sizewell 'B' and the economics of nuclear power. The CEGB suggested that the 1200-megawatt PWR station would cover its own costs in its lifetime by saving on expensive oil and coal. It would be a good thing to depend less on coal and oil.

The opposition suggested that alternative forms of energy should be explored further. Solar, wind and wave power together with coal and oil would be preferable. Economists argued which power would be the cheapest in the next century. How can anyone be sure of the price of energy in the year 2010 whether it be coal, oil or nuclear?

The inquiry started early in 1983 at a Concert Hall known as Snape Maltings, near the Sizewell site. Huge crowds followed the early days of the inquiry. Very few attended the closing stages. Also the cost to pressure groups is too great to justify being there every day for two years. The CEGB, on the other hand, have unlimited money to spend on experts of all kinds.

The second year has seen discussions on the safety of nuclear power and, in particular, the PWR. Friends of the Earth suggested the reactor was one hundred times less safe than had been stated by the CEGB. If an accident happened the cost would be between one and fifteen billion pounds. This would depend on how much radioactivity was released and on the weather at the time. Many thousands would have to leave their homes for a year. Ipswich, the county town, could be evacuated for twenty years. There would be enormous disruption to farming. The CEGB defend their case by stating that not one member of the public has died because of nuclear power in this country. Nuclear power has been with us for thirty years and it has a great safety record.

Some have argued that an AGR would be safer on the site. Certainly AGRs already work safely here. Even the South of Scotland Electricity Board argued against the PWR and for the AGR. The CEGB took note of the criticism and designed an AGR for the site just in case they failed at the inquiry. When Sizewell was first proposed for a PWR, it was to be the first of ten such reactors. Gradually the number has been reduced to five as the inquiry progressed. At least the protesters will be able to claim that they have limited the number of PWRs.

Model of Sizewell B

Suffolk Preservation Society were concerned about the local impact of a second reactor. Sizewell, they protested, is not the best site for the first PWR. The demand for electricity was not in Suffolk and the grid system to carry the electricity to other areas was not suitable. Hinkley Point in Somerset was a better site but the people there would also offer resistance to the CEGB.

As the inquiry drew to a close, CND presented their case. Their main worry was that nuclear power stations supply the plutonium for nuclear weapons. The inquiry finished on 7 March 1985. It cost the CEGB approximately ten million pounds.

The Inspector's Report, published on 26 January 1987, suggested that the PWR should go ahead at Sizewell. Government approval was given on 12 March 1987. The start of a PWR programme in Britain was sealed.

NO ESCAPE FROM SHOREHAM

A 67-metre high nuclear power station has yet to be started in Shoreham, Long Island, USA. The building is there, the storehouse contains many tonnes of uranium, but permission to start has not been granted. Some people wonder if permission will ever be granted by the Nuclear Regulatory Commission. The owners, Long Island Lighting Company, have even painted the buildings with aquamarine to blend in with the surroundings.

The owners planned a series of nuclear reactors along the shore to send power to the New England states. The Shoreham plant is all that remains of this plan; two others were defeated at public inquiries.

Long Island Lighting Company built the Shoreham plant knowing the complaints regarding the location of their PWR. Perhaps they were hoping to force the reactor on the inhabitants. It has not worked because calculations have shown that a melt-down would make Long Island uninhabitable for twenty years. This was even before the Three Mile Island melt-down had happened. Research also showed that the Island's water supply would be permanently contaminated. Shoreham suddenly seemed a most inappropriate site.

The geography of Shoreham

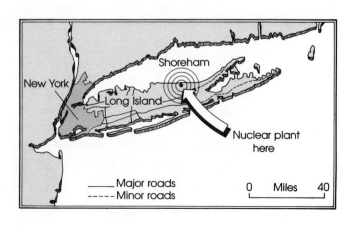

31

The roads from Shoreham to New York are usually jammed with traffic for 8 kilometres. What would happen if people needed to escape from a nuclear accident? Those on the eastern part of Long Island would have to move *closer* to the nuclear plant on evacuation. Still the owners pressed on with the 820-megawatt reactor, increasing the price of electricity by 100% to pay for it.

Environmentalists were losing the battle until the Government of Suffolk County announced that it could not approve any evacuation plan. No such plans were feasible, they said. In the meantime Shoreham nuclear plant remains idle.

OLD NUCLEAR POWER STATIONS NEVER DIE

Nuclear power stations reach the end of their working lives when the cost of keeping them efficient and safe is too high. The CEGB are formulating plans for closing down a typical Magnox station. None are yet due for closure but a three-stage process has been planned. Closing a nuclear power station is called *decommissioning*. The programme is designed so that the site remains safe at all times.

- Stage 1: The fuel rods are removed from the reactor core and the reactor is then sealed off to ensure that no radiation reaches the environment.
- Stage 2: The plant and buildings external to the reactor are dismantled. This will be done within a few years of shut-down. It will liberate valuable land for re-use. These two stages will take 10 to 15 years to complete.
- Stage 3: Total clearance of the site will depend on two factors. If there are plans to re-use the site for nuclear power this work can start quite soon. If the site is to return to public use, the level of radiation must be allowed to *die-away* to very small values. This may take a hundred years. Radioactive waste will be disposed of by methods already used in the industry.

The site would have to be guarded throughout the decommissioning process. The cost of decommissioning one Magnox station depends on the time taken for each stage. The CEGB estimate that it will cost £270 million for one Magnox station.

Old nuclear power stations never die . . . they just continue to radiate while decommissioning takes place.

Stage 1: Reactors shut down and fuel removed (The bus is shown to scale

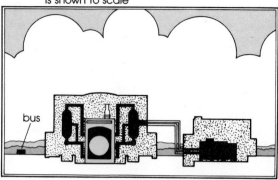

Stage 2: Reactors and concrete shielding retained, external plant and buildings removed

The three stages of decommissioning

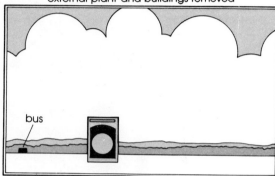

Stage 3: Total clearance

FUSION . . . THE ANSWER TO OUR ENERGY DREAMS?

So far we have seen the ways that nuclear splitting (fission) produces energy. Some atoms can be made to combine (*fusion*), and this also produces energy. Thirteenth August 1978 was a great day for energy. Scientists at Princetown University, New Jersey, USA performed the first controlled fusion experiment. This produced a temperature of 60 million degrees Celsius (centigrade) for one tenth of a second. This temperature is four times that estimated for the centre of the Sun. Interestingly, the process that produces the Sun's energy is also fusion. Fusion is also involved in the hydrogen bomb, but this is uncontrolled.

In fusion, two isotopes of hydrogen, deuterium and tritium, combine to make the element helium. They only combine at very high temperatures, but when they do, they release unbelievable amounts of energy.

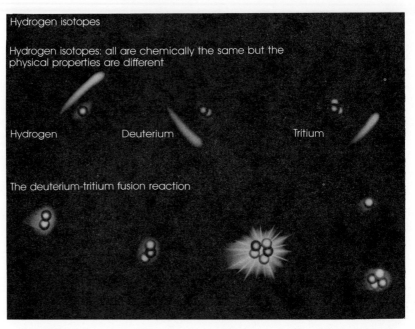

Hydrogen isotopes

Hydrogen isotopes: all are chemically the same but the physical properties are different

Hydrogen   Deuterium   Tritium

The deuterium-tritium fusion reaction

Deuterium	Tritium	fuse at very high temperature	to make	Neutron + Helium plus immense heat given out

The fusion reactor will use sea water as its source of the hydrogen isotopes. There is certainly a plentiful supply of sea-water. It is estimated that a glass of water could supply as much energy as a tonne of petrol by fusion. The difficulties are the huge temperature required and making the sort of container that can take this temperature. These difficulties mean that fusion will not be in wide use until early next century. Fusion will produce very little radiation and other pollution. It will be much 'cleaner' than the present nuclear fission used in our nuclear power stations.

Culham in Oxfordshire is a centre of excellence for nuclear research. It was chosen as the centre for fusion in Europe. Eleven other countries have combined with the UK in an attempt to produce controlled fusion. The project is called Joint European Torus, JET. The torus is the ring 'doughnut' structure which contains the fusion reaction. The fusion reaction would melt all material containers. This problem is overcome by keeping the reaction in a strong magnetic field. The magnetism holds the fusion reaction in its place at the centre of the torus. It is said to be kept in a 'magnetic bottle'.

The immense heat generated by the fusion process is conducted away by a blanket of the element lithium. The hot lithium blanket then heats water and converts it into steam. The steam drives a turbine which makes electricity. Fusion could well be the answer to our energy problems in the 21st century.

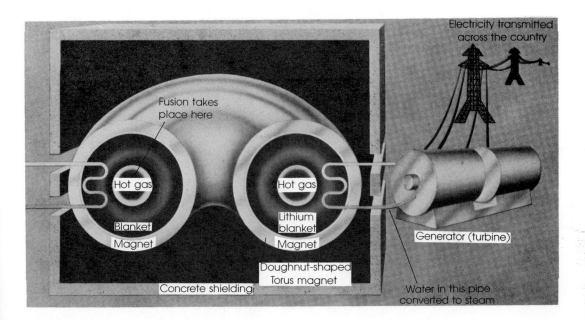

A fusion reactor

QUESTIONS ON CHAPTER 2

In questions 1–3, supply words to fill in the blanks. Do not write on this page.

1 Fusion involves _____ isotopes combining at very high _____ . The process is the same as that producing the heat and the _____ on the _____ ; this energy gives us life on _____ . It is a '_____' process giving out little _____ to harm us.

2 The _____ reactor planned for Sizewell is similar to the _____ _____ Island one. This is the _____ for all the fuss.

3 Old power stations of the nuclear type must be _____ by _____ stages. The first involves _____ of the rods and _____ off the reactor. The third stage depends on whether the site is to be _____ or not. The level of _____ is the _____ factor on how _____ this stage will last.

4 How does nuclear power compare with coal as a fuel?

5 Why can nuclear power be labelled 'honey-venom'?

6 What do moderators and coolants do in nuclear reactors?

7 What are the similarities and differences when comparing an oil-fired power station with a nuclear one?

8 How many nuclear power plants are there in Britain today? Look at the map on page 25 and discuss the distribution of these power stations.

9 What is a 'melt-down' in a nuclear reactor? How did it happen at Three Mile Island?

10 The Three Mile Island accident shook the nuclear power industry. What effect did it have?

11 How can a fast reactor be modified to make it a breeder?

12 The following are questions about the Sizewell 'B' inquiry.
(a) What type of reactor is the inquiry about?
(b) The inquiry has lasted two years. Why is it so important?
(c) What have been the major arguments over the two years?
(d) Do you think the cost of the inquiry is justified? Explain your reasoning.

13 Why is the Shoreham, Long Island, site unsuitable for a reactor?

14 The world's worst nuclear accident happened at Chernobyl on 25 April 1986. Now that further information has come to light, complete the story by discovering:
(a) the number of casualties;
(b) the extent of radiation damage to crops and soil in the area;
(c) the damage caused to other European countries by fall-out;
(d) the effect of the incident on the nuclear programmes in Russia and other countries.

How much worse would the accident have been if a full melt-down had taken place?

Has anything good come out of this accident?

WORDFINDER ON NUCLEAR POWER STATIONS

First, trace this grid on to a piece of paper (or photocopy this page – teacher, please see the note at the front of the book). Then solve the following clues and put a ring around the answers. Answers go in any direction: across, back, up, down and diagonally. Do not write on this page. The answer to the first question has been ringed to help you.

J	S	E	P	F	J	D	I	S	T	U	D
R	W	P	L	A	N	O	R	T	U	E	N
O	L	N	L	S	C	M	G	X	C	F	J
W	F	Q	E	T	N	A	L	O	O	C	T
P	B	O	W	R	L	N	M	S	T	M	V
A	U	T	E	L	Y	M	A	G	N	O	X
N	C	V	Z	L	I	D	L	E	M	N	Y
I	D	A	I	S	C	O	J	B	G	E	C
A	W	T	S	M	A	U	D	F	H	V	F
H	G	I	Z	U	G	F	U	E	L	R	W
C	O	A	L	N	R	B	E	K	V	A	T
N	S	R	O	T	A	R	E	D	O	M	H

1 In the nucleus of atoms (7)
2 Something that burns (4)
3 A gas-cooled reactor (3)
4 Nuclear reactor more controversial than most (3)
5 When a nuclear plant has finished its useful life ____ it (12)
6 Takes the heat out of the reactor core (7)
7 A type of reactor involving a magnesium alloy (6)
8 The electricity people (4)
9 European project for fusion (3)
10 A poor fuel when compared with nuclear ones (4)
11 Keeps the neutrons in check in a reactor (9)
12 There is absolutely no danger (4)
13 Subject of a two-year inquiry (8)
14 A quicker sort of reactor (4)
15 Three Mile Island remains ____ today (4)
16 Uranium is honey-____ (5)
17 America (3)
18 The fission of uranium is a ____ reaction (5)

CHAPTER 3

NUCLEAR WASTE

WHAT IS INVOLVED IN REPROCESSING?

All nuclear power stations use rods of fuel encased in metal. When the rods have finished their useful life in the reactor, they are taken to the reprocessing plant. The metal containers are cut open and the contents dissolved in acid. The resulting solution is then given chemical treatment. Any gases formed in this process are filtered to remove solids and then released to the air. The gases have only low radioactivity.

The sources of nuclear waste in the nuclear industry

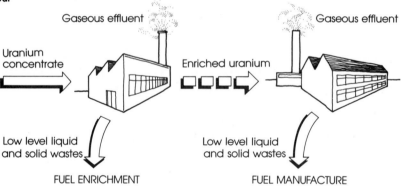

Gaseous effluent

Uranium concentrate

Gaseous effluent

Enriched uranium

Low level liquid and solid wastes

FUEL ENRICHMENT

Low level liquid and solid wastes

FUEL MANUFACTURE

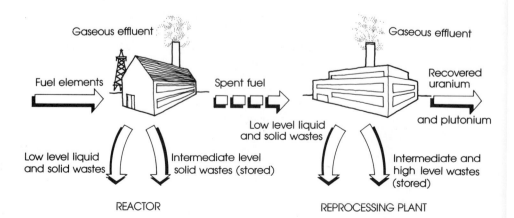

Gaseous effluent

Fuel elements

Gaseous effluent

Spent fuel

Recovered uranium

Low level liquid and solid wastes

and plutonium

Low level liquid and solid wastes

Intermediate level solid wastes (stored)

Intermediate and high level wastes (stored)

REACTOR

REPROCESSING PLANT

The solution, made by adding the acid, is concentrated and stored in cooled tanks to solidify. Other radioactive solids and liquids arise from the metal containers, cooling waters, and various liquids used in the chemical processes. Low-level liquid wastes are discharged into the sea. The valuable uranium and plutonium, obtained by the chemical processes, is kept. This will fuel future reactors.

DISPOSAL OF NUCLEAR WASTE

There are various types of nuclear waste and they are graded by the degree of their radioactivity

- Low level waste: Radioactivity low enough to allow direct disposal to the environment. Huge volumes of this are produced.
- Intermediate level waste: Medium level of radioactivity. There are large volumes of it.
- High level waste: A high level of radioactivity. It gives out a lot of heat. Small volumes of this are produced.

The wastes may come from uranium mining, reprocessing, or the nuclear power station itself. The pictures on the page opposite show the different types of waste coming from reactors, reprocessing, fuel enrichment and manufacture.

Nuclear wastes must be disposed of according to the degree of their radioactivity. The pictures opposite show disposal methods and the following notes will help in understanding them.

Land disposal of low level solid waste

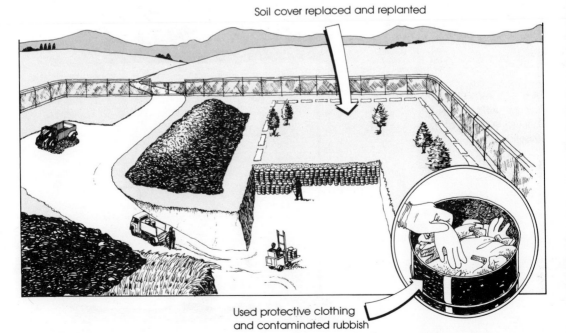

Soil cover replaced and replanted

Used protective clothing and contaminated rubbish

Low level wastes

Land disposal

The waste is mainly laboratory equipment and protective clothing. In the UK most of it is stored at Drigg near Sellafield in Cumbria. The waste is placed in trenches over a natural layer of clay. The clay prevents radioactivity seeping away should corrosion of the metal containers take place.

Deep sea disposal

The solid wastes are of higher activity than those stored at Drigg. They are from hospitals, university laboratories and factories. The wastes are cast into concrete. The concrete is surrounded by steel drums. The concrete and steel protect the workers handling the waste and ensure that the drums reach the sea bottom in one piece. This method of disposal is banned in the UK at the moment.

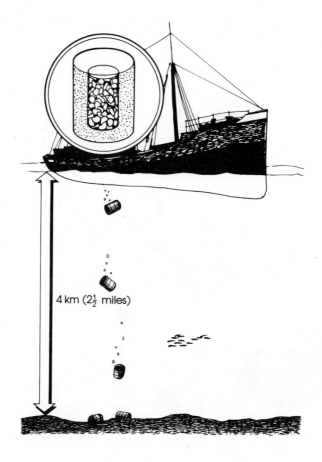

Deep sea disposal of low level solid wastes (banned in the UK at present)

4 km ($2\frac{1}{2}$ miles)

Sea disposal

This is for liquid wastes such as the ponds used to store spent fuel. The ponds are next to the power station. They are water-filled and nuclear waste is stored below the water until its radioactivity has dropped far enough for safer disposal elsewhere, at sea for example. This method is also used for some liquids from the reprocessing plant. The liquids are simply fed into the sea about 1.6 kilometres out. Trawsfynydd reactor discharges into a lake.

Sea disposal of low level liquid wastes

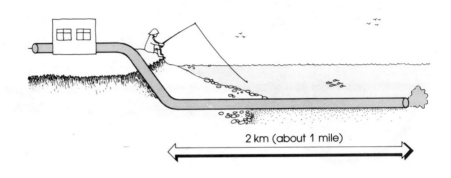

2 km (about 1 mile)

Atmospheric disposal of gaseous wastes (low level waste)

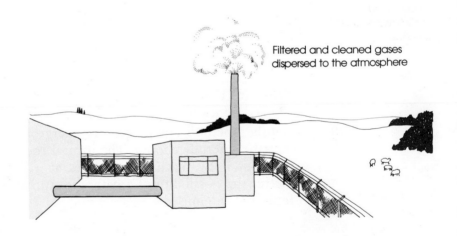

Filtered and cleaned gases dispersed to the atmosphere

Intermediate level wastes

Land disposal

Relatively large quantities of intermediate waste are produced from the making of nuclear power. Two methods of land disposal are being developed in the UK. One involves casting drums of the waste in concrete and then surrounding these

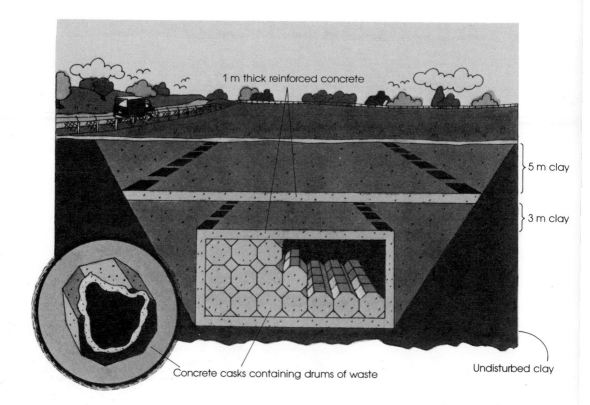

1 m thick reinforced concrete

5 m clay

3 m clay

Concrete casks containing drums of waste

Undisturbed clay

**Disposal of inter-
mediate level wastes
in shallow engineered
trenches**

slabs with two more layers of reinforced concrete. Clay on the top and beneath prevent any water getting to the waste area. Another method involves deep underground burial. The site must be carefully chosen. The natural rock must be of the right kind. By placing the wastes at a depth of about 300 metres the possibility of a natural disturbance or human interference is minimised.

High level wastes

Storage tanks for liquids

The liquid wastes are kept in stainless steel tanks which are contained in concrete vaults further lined inside with steel. Heat is removed by several sets of cooling coils. An agitator mixes the waste and helps loss of heat.

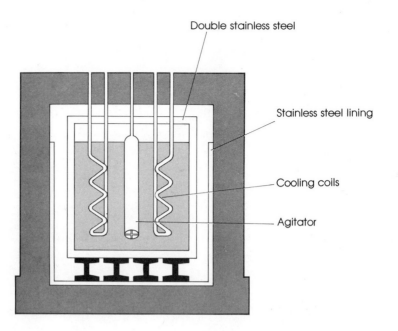

Double stainless steel

Stainless steel lining

Storage tank for high level liquid wastes

Cooling coils

Agitator

Solidification in glass

High level wastes in liquid form are difficult to store. The idea of making the liquid waste into a solid is attractive. In the 1960s liquid waste was sealed into glass. This is called *vitrification*. The glass survives the effects of heat and radiation undamaged. The French use this method and British Nuclear Fuels Ltd, BNFL, will use it in 1990. The vitrified waste is stored in steel canisters containing concrete. They can be kept in a surface store or buried.

Deep underground disposal

The vitrified waste is surrounded by a metal canister which is further surrounded by absorbent material. This is placed into a shaft of rock 500 metres below the Earth's surface.

Ocean bed disposal

There are large areas of deep ocean bed where the sediments have been undisturbed for millions of years. The waste containers with vitrified waste, concrete and steel, could be placed amongst this sediment, but this method is not used yet.

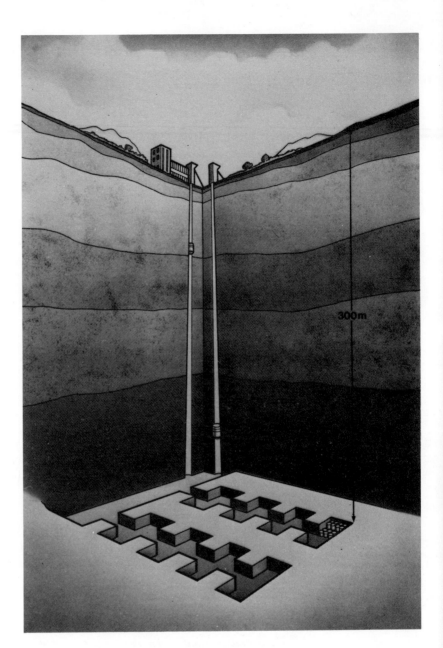

Disposal of inter-
mediate level wastes
in deep underground
chambers. High level
wastes stored similarly
but at a greater depth
(500 metres)

300m

SELLAFIELD: THE NUCLEAR LAUNDRY

Sellafield is on the Cumbrian coast of north-west England.
The site houses a nuclear reprocessing plant and nuclear
reactors. It used to be called Windscale and such is its fame
that it is still often referred to by that name. You can see the
position of the Sellafield plant on the map in Chapter 2.

Sellafield reprocesses nuclear waste from the sixteen UK nuclear reactors and some similar waste from Japan. Some of the waste is pumped into the Irish Sea. The sea surrounding Sellafield contains a quarter of a tonne of radioactive plutonium. A millionth of a gram of plutonium can cause human cancer. The sea will remain intensely radioactive for a quarter of a million years.

The spent fuel sent to Sellafield contains a lot of uranium and a little plutonium. There are also small amounts of highly radioactive waste. The plutonium and uranium can be used again and so these are extracted at Sellafield. The rest is useless but highly dangerous because of its radioactivity. Sellafield can reprocess 1500 tonnes of used fuel a year. This quantity only yields 3 tonnes of plutonium. The most dangerous waste is stored on site. The rest is sent into the sea by pipeline.

The Sellafield nuclear complex from the west

There seem to be ten-times more childhood cancers in the Sellafield area than is average for the country. Some of this cancer might be caused by radiation. Radiation has been shown to cause cancer in animals. Experts point out that there are other areas with high cancer figures. These areas have no such extra radiation. The serious worries in most recent times have been about the pipeline waste.

45

There have been accidents at Sellafield over a period of 30 years:

1952–83	Quarter of a tonne of plutonium discharged to sea
1957	Fire in No 1 plutonium production reactor
1970	Plutonium goes 'critical' in recovery plant
1973	Blow-back in B204 'head-end' reprocessing plant
1974	Car park found to be radioactive
1975	Radioactive cobalt and caesium found in River Calder
1976	Major leak from silo B38 discovered
1978	Hydrogen build-up threatens explosion
	Seven-year-old leak found from building B701
1979	Uranium ignites in fuel decanning plant
	Fire in B204, now disused
1981	Radioactive iodine released from building 205
1983	Beach closed by radioactive slick
1986	Plutonium escaped into the atmosphere
	1,100 litres of radioactive waste escape from a fractured pipe
	Team of Government inspectors sent to Sellafield to inquire into safety aspects (full inquiry)

Greenpeace is an environmental group that chooses to protect our environment by direct action. Their action is often made in dangerous conditions and involves great bravery. Perhaps it is this bravery that has caught the imagination of so many. In November 1983 Greenpeace tried to block the waste pipeline at Sellafield. They dived from an inflatable dinghy at the point where the waste leaves the pipeline. They failed because BNFL had been tipped off about the raid and had moved the pipeline. Greenpeace made a second attempt, breaking the law this time. Two of their divers were seriously contaminated with radiation. Greenpeace were fined £40 000 for breaking the law. Greenpeace had at least focused public attention on the Sellafield pipeline.

On 1 December 1983 highly contaminated seaweed was washed up in large amounts on the beaches near Sellafield. Miles of beach were officially closed to members of the public. The summer of 1984 was a lean time for hotels and guest houses. The local beaches had been popular for bathing in the past. Nobody seemed to want the added ingredient of radioactivity in their holiday. The owners of these holiday houses decided to try to claim lost earnings from BNFL. Meanwhile the Government's Director of Public Prosecutions decided that BNFL could be prosecuted for allowing excessive radioactive leaks from the pipeline.

When the Sellafield reprocessing plant was first started, scientists thought that the radioactive waste would attach itself to the muddy silt at the bottom of the Ravenglass estuary. They did not reckon on the silt gradually moving towards Scotland in the way that it has.

The western coast of Scotland with its many islands is polluted with the radiation. Some of the radioactive silt has been found in Greenland and Norway. Part of the northern tip of Ireland is also affected. The Irish have asked for the pipeline waste to be stopped.

More evidence has come to light regarding cancer local to Sellafield. Such is the concern that Sir Douglas Black, a well-known doctor, was appointed to head an inquiry. The inquiry showed a higher incidence of some types of cancer but suggested that there was no proven link with radiation. Environmentalists were sceptical about the findings 'unproven link'. BNFL say that the small amounts of radiation given out from Sellafield could never account for cancer. Many eminent people agree with them. BNFL have recently announced that they are to reduce the radioactivity issuing from the pipeline.

The report of an all-party select committee looking into the UK's nuclear industry was published on 12 March 1986. It contained some harsh words on Sellafield. Sellafield produces the 'largest recorded source of radioactive discharge in the world'. The radioactivity 'has a nasty habit of concentrating around our shores and in our seafood'. The committee felt that there may not be a good case for continuing reprocessing as the price of nuclear fuel had dropped considerably.

It is a worrying time for the families living close to Sellafield. They are told that it is dangerous to eat fish caught locally. Scientists have found traces of plutonium in the dust collected by vacuum cleaners in the homes around Sellafield. Local people dare not use the beaches or swim in the sea. Will their children develop cancer? Should they move from the area? Who will buy their houses in such an area? Such fear cannot continue; the inquiry, we hope, will calm their fears.

NUCLEAR COCKTAIL?

Is enough care taken over the choice of an area for nuclear waste dumping? Today's guidelines say that the waste site is to be considered as the *only* source of radiation. Surely when the site is suggested, other sources of radiation should be considered.

Consider Sellafield, which should not be used as a nuclear waste site as it already has more than its share of radiation from the nuclear power station there. People there already suffer radiation from the air, dust, local crops, local meat from cows and sheep, direct contact with sediments on the

Spent nuclear fuel
leaving Hunterston B
nuclear power station
for Sellafield

beach and radioactivity from the nuclear power stations. Any
industry using coal-fired heating also produces some radioactivity. Industries using high temperature kilns also give off
radiation. It is the total nuclear cocktail that counts.

BUGS IN THE NUCLEAR BIN?

Plans are afoot to bury highly radioactive waste very deeply
under the ground. Will microbes, living things only visible
through a microscope, eat into the materials containing the
waste? Worse still, will they bring the radioactivity to the
surface and contaminate us? This sounds like the stuff of
science fiction.

A team of scientists at Harwell's Institute of Geological
Science feel that microbes may be able to do just this. Past
research shows that microbes may be able to live near high-
level nuclear waste. Many organisms are highly tolerant of
radiation. Some microbes live deep in mines and wells; they
also corrode things there. Other microbes will withstand
temperatures of 104°C and pressures one thousand times that
of the atmosphere. Perhaps the idea is not so silly after all.

VILLAGE FIGHTS WASTE

The true voice of the nation is often said to be in the village
hall. Certainly Elstow, a sleepy village in Bedfordshire, has
been having its share of village meetings.

The government has chosen Elstow as a possible site to store nuclear waste. They wish to use shallow burial for the waste at Elstow. The geography of the area is ideal. There is a thick layer of clay near the surface and this will prevent water reaching the waste and spreading it. The density of the clay also helps to keep the radiation in check.

Many local people do not want nuclear waste in their village. It is a problem that nobody wants. How can the planners convince us that a nuclear dump is safe? We cannot see, smell or touch radiation. This adds to the mystery and fear.

NUCLEAR DUMPING AT SEA ENDS

Greenpeace, the environmental activists, have long campaigned against ocean dumping of low level nuclear waste. They have pressed their case on land by informing Members of Parliament. They have pressed their case at sea by bravely blocking the path of waste drums. Early in 1983 Greenpeace worked from a fast, small inflatable dinghy. They weaved close to the ship trying to dump the waste. Some of the heavy drums dropped very close to them in the sea. The dinghy capsised several times. All of this took place some 800 kilometres off Land's End.

In August 1983 the National Union of Seamen and other unions refused to take part in dumping nuclear waste into the sea. This meant that no more nuclear waste could be dumped at sea again from Britain. This was the result for which Greenpeace had been campaigning.

The dumped material was only low level waste; clothing and lightly contaminated equipment from atomic weapons research.

Government Ministers still feel the waste is so slightly contaminated, and the ocean so large, that there is no danger. The environmental groups know this is true but they have a long-term interest. They want to stop the dumping of more highly radioactive waste at sea in the future.

TRANSPORT OF NUCLEAR WASTE ON LAND

In the UK, nuclear waste is transported by rail. Special flasks are used for the purpose. They are made of steel 350 mm thick. They weigh 50 tonnes and can contain 200 spent fuel rods. The flasks are filled with water to take the heat from the rods to the fins. The fins lose this heat to the atmosphere.

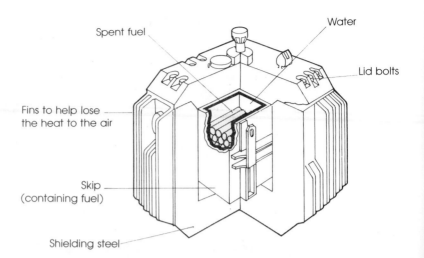

Spent fuel

Water

Spent fuel
transport flask

Fins to help lose
the heat to the air

Lid bolts

Skip
(containing fuel)

Shielding steel

These flasks must be able to withstand any possible accident. In tests they drop the flasks on to hard surfaces from a height of 9 metres. They also engulf the flask in fire to reach temperatures of 800° Celsius. In a further test they immerse the flask in a 15-metre depth of water. The story of one spectacular test follows.

Loco's last run

In the mid-summer of 1984 a worldwide TV audience of millions watched a diesel train on its last run. It was due to be scrapped and this was definitely its last journey. At 140 tonnes, it was one of the heaviest type used by British Rail. It pulled three coaches, each weighing 35 tonnes. There were no people on board and it was operated automatically.

Flask in position for
the crash

The train left Edwalton, in Nottinghamshire, and after 12.8 kilometres it had reached 160 kph. This more than equalled the impact that a high speed train would make at 200 kph.

When it reached Old Dalby in Leicestershire, the train struck a nuclear fuel flask. The flask had been placed in its worst imaginable position. The crash was spectacular. There was a devastating explosion of fire and flame. It took 5 seconds for flask, train and coaches to come to rest. The locomotive was crushed. What a way to end its days! The carriages were badly damaged. The point of the demonstration had been made . . . the nuclear fuel flask was completely intact.

The crash

Why did the CEGB stage this crash? There had been much public concern about the transport of nuclear waste. Though there was an excellent safety record the message was not getting across. In more than 7000 journeys on British Rail's network there had been no accidents involving loss of radio-activity. Nevertheless, the CEGB felt that this train crash was necessary to prove their point. Sir Walter Marshall, Chairman of the CEGB, was quickly on the scene to view the flask. He told the world's press, 'In the past people have had to take our word that these flasks are safe. Now they can see for themselves'.

Not everyone was satisfied. Greenpeace claimed that the flask should have been placed with the vulnerable lid facing the train. This would expose the weakness of the flask.

QUESTIONS ON CHAPTER 3

In questions 1–4, supply words to fill in the blanks. Do not write on this page.

1 Spent fuel rods are ＿＿ to regain ＿＿ and ＿＿ which may be used to ＿＿ future reactors.

2 The ＿＿ site near Sellafield is used for ＿＿-＿＿ nuclear waste. The natural ＿＿ of ＿＿ protects the waste from ＿＿ and corrosion.

3 The nuclear waste flasks are made of ＿＿ . They weigh ＿＿ and usually carry up to ＿＿ fuel rods. Water ＿＿ the heat to the atmosphere via metal ＿＿ .

4 The village of ＿＿ in the county of ＿＿ is fighting against ＿＿ ＿＿ being dumped on their land. The area is highly suitable because of the thick natural layer of ＿＿ . This cuts down the ＿＿ and the ＿＿ .

5 Describe the three types of nuclear waste and say where these wastes might come from.

6 Describe the methods of land disposal for the various types of nuclear waste.

7 What are the advantages of mixing liquid waste with glass?

8 How are liquid nuclear wastes disposed of?

9 Describe tests that have been made to demonstrate the safety of nuclear waste flasks.

10 On what grounds did Greenpeace object to the express train collision with a nuclear flask?

11 The people from Sellafield are subjected to a 'nuclear cocktail'. What does this mean? Is it fair on the local residents?

12 Why has nuclear dumping at sea been stopped in the United Kingdom? What contribution did Greenpeace play?

13 What evidence is there to support the idea of bugs attacking nuclear waste?

14 The following are questions about Sellafield.
(a) Why is it called the nuclear laundry?
(b) What are the fears about the waste in the Irish Sea?
(c) What is happening about the high cancer figures?

4

BOMBS AND MISSILES

HOW NUCLEAR BOMBS WORK

The destructive power of a bomb is always compared with tri-nitro-toluene, TNT, an early chemical explosive with considerable powers of destruction. A 1-megatonne explosion means that the destruction is equal to that made by 1 000 000 tonnes of TNT. These can be made from uranium or plutonium.

The atom bomb

The isotope of uranium known as uranium-235, is very unusual. It cannot be kept in large lumps or it automatically explodes. The smallest size that explodes is called the *critical mass*. This size is estimated to be about ten kilograms (10 000 grams).

The atom bomb

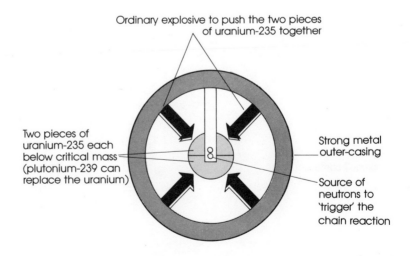

Ordinary explosive to push the two pieces of uranium-235 together

Two pieces of uranium-235 each below critical mass (plutonium-239 can replace the uranium)

Strong metal outer-casing

Source of neutrons to 'trigger' the chain reaction

When the uranium does explode, it is the same chain reaction as in the nuclear reactor. The main difference is that it is not controlled. The atom bomb consists of two pieces of uranium-235 below critical mass. These two pieces are brought together violently by a detonator. The detonator is usually a small charge of TNT. The chain reaction takes place so fast that huge temperatures and pressures are generated. Dangerous radioactive material is widely distributed as *fall-out*. Gamma-radiation, by far the most harmful, is given out in abundance. The Hiroshima atom bomb was the first to be used in war. It was followed a few days later by an atom bomb made of plutonium-239. This bomb was dropped on the Japanese city of Nagasaki. The Second World War ended a few days later.

The hydrogen bomb

The atom bomb was thought to be rather limited in its destructive power. The reason was that the pieces of uranium or plutonium could not be bigger than the critical size. If they were bigger the bomb would explode immediately. The hydrogen, or H-, bomb was the solution to this problem. It contained an atom bomb, at its centre. The atoms of uranium split up by fission (described on p. 20). The neutrons given off from the fission reacted with a compound called lithium deuteride. The deuteride part is an isotope of hydrogen, hence hydrogen bomb. A further process called fusion takes place. This is described on p. 33. The energy given out is enormous. The total energy is from the fission and fusion processes. The hydrogen bomb is sometimes called a 'clean' one because it gives out harmless helium gas. But the atom bomb at its centre gives out radiation, and it can therefore hardly claim the title 'clean'.

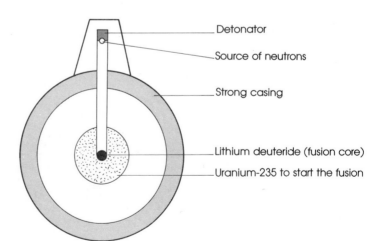

The hydrogen bomb

Detonator

Source of neutrons

Strong casing

Lithium deuteride (fusion core)

Uranium-235 to start the fusion

An improvement on this bomb is the fission–fusion–fission type of hydrogen bomb. It has an additional layer of natural uranium around it. This reacts with the neutrons to give even more energy.

The neutron bomb

This is a modified hydrogen bomb. It is specially designed so that very little of its energy is given out as heat and blast. The energy is concentrated to give out an enormous burst of neutron radiation.

Neutrons are the most penetrating of all radiations and will pass through tanks and people. People soon die from this radiation. The lack of blast means that buildings remain intact. The destruction is limited to living things.

The neutron bomb consists of a very small atom bomb at one end. Lithium tritide is at the other end. The tritide is from an isotope of hydrogen. The bomb is surrounded by a case of polythene and an outer casing of beryllium metal. The small atom bomb of uranium gives out intense X-rays which turn the polythene into a hot gas. This gas compresses the lithium tritide to many times its usual density. Fusion then takes place and a very high yield of neutrons is given out. The beryllium casing produces more neutrons when hit by them. This multiplies the number of neutrons given out.

THE BOMB CONNECTION

Nuclear power stations supply many of us with electricity. The power can be relatively cheap and clean. Some countries have been helped by richer countries to build their own nuclear power stations. Nuclear power stations require uranium or plutonium as fuel. These are the same substances that are used to make atomic and hydrogen bombs.

There is a great worry that too many countries now have such bombs. They could use the fuel for their nuclear power stations for bombs as well. The more countries that have the bomb, the greater the chance of nuclear war. The leaders of some countries are not as responsible as others. A national leader could threaten a nuclear attack and just *might* carry it out. The process where more and more countries are becoming nuclear powers is called *proliferation*. The more countries involved, the more difficult it is to get agreement. Perhaps in the future, poorer countries will demand food for their people by threatening nuclear attack. Surely the ultimate threat?

The Russian arsenal of nuclear weapons is about the same size as the American one. This means that together they have about 45 000 nuclear weapons. The arsenals of the other three nuclear powers, China, France and the United Kingdom, total about 2000 nuclear warheads. This means that there are three tonnes of TNT for every man, woman and child on Earth.

This is equivalent to over a million Hiroshima bombs. The nuclear arsenals are much larger than could ever be used. This is why Russia and America regularly have arms limitation talks. It is hard for these talks to produce anything very useful as the distrust between the powers is too great.

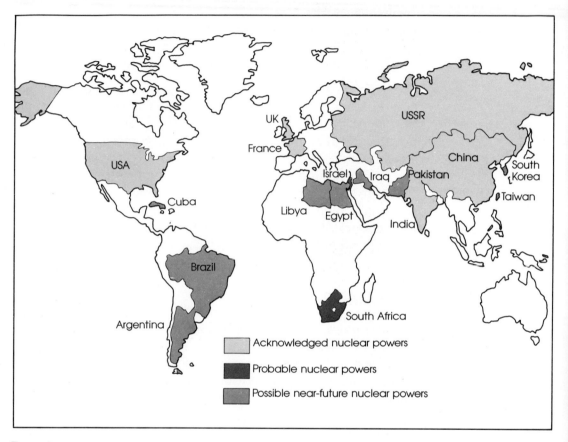

The nuclear powers –
who has the bomb?

ATOMIC DESTRUCTION

Father Johannes Siemes, a priest, lived just one mile from Hiroshima in Japan. The Second World War was nearing its end. They were used to air raids near Hiroshima and so the alarm on 6 August 1945 was no surprise. It was 7.00 am on a bright summer's day. The view from Father Siemes' window looked down the valley towards the city of Hiroshima.

A bright yellow light lit up the whole valley. There seemed to be a wave of heat. There followed a loud explosion. Window frames and doors were shot from the houses. Glass fragments were everywhere. Houses and woods were aflame down the valley. There was a state of confusion all around.

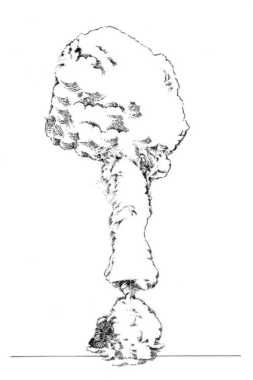

A mushroom cloud

Father Siemes and some of his fellow priests were lucky. They only had minor cuts. They went to help their neighbours. Some of these spoke about seeing three planes high over the city at the time of the explosion. There was a huge column of smoke over the city.

About half an hour after the explosion, an endless procession of burnt and bleeding people came up the valley. They were escaping the destruction. Soon the first-aid supplies had run out. Who could prepare for such a huge disaster? News reached them that the entire city had been destroyed and was on fire. What could be done?

In the evening Father Siemes and others walked into the city. There were screams from people trapped below the rubble of their houses as flames drew closer. They had to be left to die. There were too many problems and no facilities left for rescue.

Survivors could see permanent *shadows* on the streets. The intense heat made people change into gases. Their bodies had concentrated the heat and left burn marks, known as shadows, on the street.

As if this was not enough, in the evening they saw a whirlwind in the city park. It uprooted trees and lifted them high into the air. It also took a water spout 100 metres high from a lake. Some, already injured, were drowned by the water sent high into the air.

'Shadows' of those
close to the Hiroshima
bomb

The darkness of the evening was never more welcome. It hid
the horrors of the city. The day after started with a frightful
picture of ashes and ruin. Piles of dead bodies were being
burnt to prevent the spread of disease. The smell was almost
unbearable.

They were soon to learn what had caused this massive destruction. It was the first atom bomb ever to be dropped. The uranium
in the bomb exploded to give great heat and light. The
explosive force had flattened nearby houses and taken windows
and doors out of others. The gamma-radiation caused most of
the horrific burns. The official death toll by 1 September was
70 000 and 130 000 wounded.

Father Siemes died 38 years later on the same day that the
bomb had dropped.

What is the situation today in Hiroshima? Many more have
died of radiation sickness, cancer and other long term
illnesses. Their deaths were so painful that it was said that
'the dying envied the dead'. Official figures now place the
total dead at 200 000. A few days later an atom bomb
dropped on Nagasaki, another Japanese city. Some of the
victims were burnt so badly by the radiation that even plastic
surgery failed to hide their disfigurement. Some have been
heard to say that they wish they had died in the bomb blast.

The destruction of Hiroshima has given rise to much
controversy. Some people claim that it shortened the war,
saving large numbers of casualties and freeing many prisoners
of war. Others claim that the war could have ended without
the suffering that the bomb caused.

Japan: the atom bomb targets

A chilling thought ... today's bombs are thousands of times more powerful than those that fell on Hiroshima and Nagasaki. It follows that many more would die.

WHEN THE BOMB DROPS

When a nuclear bomb drops it gives out its energy in three ways. There is the shock or blast wave caused by the rapid chain explosion, which flattens all in its path. There is an intense heat wave which will set fire to anything combustible and cause serious burns to humans. The pulse of gamma-rays given out by the bomb ruins electrical and electronic equipment and stops communications. This is called the *nuclear electro-magnetic pulse*, NEP. Lastly there is the radiation which destroys living things.

Roughly half of the energy of the bomb goes into the shock wave. One-third of the energy goes into the intense heat wave. The remaining ten per cent of the energy goes into the nuclear radiation. The damage inflicted does depend on where the bomb explodes. It may be an air burst or a ground burst. A 1-megatonne air explosion would flatten all trees and most buildings within an area of 14 165 hectares. It would also force thousands of tons of water into the upper atmosphere.

59

A 1-megatonne ground blast would make a crater over 405 hectares. It would send 50 000 tonnes of rock and soil into the upper atmosphere as dust. Fires would cover an area of 337 square kilometres. 5000 tonnes of air would be converted into nitrogen oxides. These would cause smog on the Earth's surface and attack the ozone layer in the outer atmosphere. Without the ozone layer, we would all be in danger of 'burning up' in the Sun's rays. The ozone acts as a necessary filter for the Sun's rays.

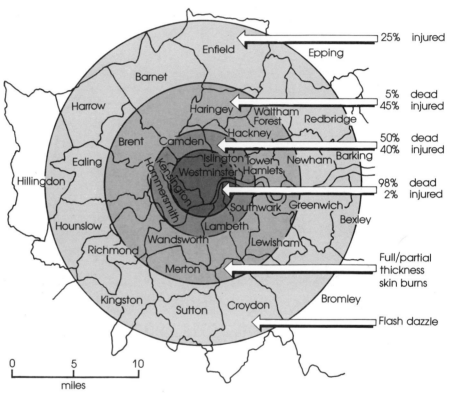

Some effects of a
1-megatonne nuclear
air-burst over the
centre of London
(Effects of fall-out are
ignored here; the
effects are long term)

BROKEN ARROW

American B47 bombers were a common sight at RAF Lakenheath in Cambridgeshire. The United States Air Force were based there as part of the protection given to the western nations by the North Atlantic Treaty Organisation, NATO.

A B47 bomber landed at Lakenheath on 27 July 1956 and immediately went out of control. It crashed into a storage igloo and burst into flames. The fire fighters concentrated on defending the igloo with large quantities of foam. The B47 crew were burnt to death. Fortunately the bomber was unarmed on its flight. There is a difference of opinion on the contents of the igloo. A retired US Air Force General who had worked at Lakenheath at the time, claims that the igloo contained nuclear bombs; three Mark 6 nuclear bombs 3.66 metres long and 1.83 metres in diameter, to be precise. The US government deny that nuclear material was there. If it was, this is the only known accident involving nuclear weapons in the UK. Such an accident is code-named a 'broken arrow'.

The fire is said to have spread inside the igloo. Once there, it badly burnt the bomb casings. Each bomb contained 8 tonnes of TNT as a trigger mechanism. If the fire had ignited the TNT the nuclear bombs would have exploded. Part of eastern England would have been reduced to desert. The whole frightening episode is surrounded with secrecy.

'Broken Arrow' rehearsal

The United States decided to rehearse their first nuclear accident in 1976.

The location for the rehearsal was the Nevada nuclear test site. A model of a Californian town was built. It included a baseball field, bar, commercial offices and a school. An army helicopter loaded with three nuclear bombs covered the town with radium-223. The radium is mild compared to plutonium, the likely source of real contamination. The radium served the purpose, as radiation clothing was necessary to handle it. The drama lasted seven days. The police, health and emergency chiefs were involved. A lot was learnt from this overdue exercise.

The American Defense Department admitted 32 'broken arrow' accidents had actually happened to date. Two of the accidents were particularly worrying. In Palomares, Southern Spain, in 1966, a B52 bomber dropped four hydrogen bombs accidentally. Eleven hundred tonnes of soil contaminated by plutonium had to be shipped to US dumps. In 1962 another B52 bomber was involved. It crashed in North Carolina and part of the uranium core of a bomb was lost. It was never recovered and formed part of a 24-megatonne atom bomb. Such a bomb is about 800 times the strength of the Hiroshima one. It is said that a single switch prevented the bomb exploding. A chilling thought.

NUCLEAR TESTS

Bombs must be tested if they are to be improved. Nuclear bombs have to be tested as far away from human populations as possible. The UK chose the Australian desert for their atomic tests in the 1950s. France and the US chose islands in the South Pacific. In all cases the test sites remain monuments to the nuclear age and human folly.

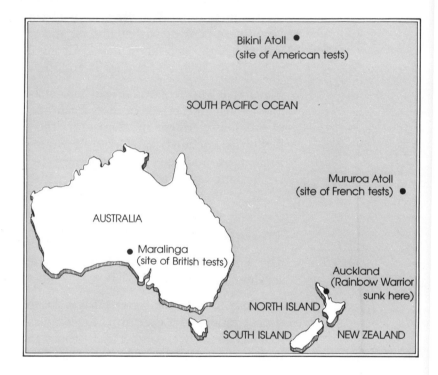

Test sites in the South Pacific

British tests

Nuclear tests were carried out in Maralinga, Australia between 1952 and 1956. British and Australian forces were involved in the tests. Today, it is claimed that 300 servicemen were used as 'guinea pigs' during one atom bomb test. The men were too close to the bomb. They were 8 kilometres from the explosion of a 20-kilotonne bomb. This was about the size of the Hiroshima bomb. Three days after, 100 members were taken into the contamination area. After tests in the area, the men were decontaminated. The Australian government claims compensation for lost lives as a result of radiation received in these tests. The case continues today.

In another test, Aborigine tribesmen were directly in the path of nuclear fall-out. There are claims that there have been terrible burns and radiation sickness amongst the Aborigines.

French tests

The South Pacific island of Mururoa suffered over 80 nuclear explosions between 1966 and 1982. The islanders were used to fishing for their food and gathering their own fruit. Today these food sources have disappeared. They live on tinned beans and corned beef. Their local food has been polluted.

There have been various accidents on the island. There was an explosion and fire in an underground laboratory. Two people were killed. Officials said that the explosion was not nuclear. However, the clean-up operation seemed to involve radiation procedures.

In another accident, a blast device got stuck under coral. Rather than try to release it, the French exploded it. The blast was so great that a crack 2 kilometres long appeared in the island's surface.

Deadly plutonium was scattered on a beach in yet another accident. Rather than clean it up, they covered it in asphalt and used the area as a nuclear dump. Unfortunately, violent storms broke up the asphalt surface and released the radiation.

In July 1985 the Greenpeace flagship *Rainbow Warrior* was blown up. It was at its berth in Auckland harbour, New Zealand. The *Warrior* had been due to lead a flotilla of ships protesting at French nuclear tests on Mururoa atoll in the Pacific.

Why would anyone wish to blow up this ship? Investigations led to a husband and wife team being detained. Sophie and Alain Turenge, the couple involved, were said to be members of the French Secret Service. Could it be that this service disliked the prying eyes of the Greenpeace environmental group?

The French President took the suggestion seriously by ordering an inquiry immediately. Greenpeace had new sensitive instruments on board the *Warrior*. These could detect neutron bomb tests. Interestingly, the French were said to be due to test neutron bombs in Mururoa.

The relations between France and South Pacific countries were already strained. Too many nuclear bombs had polluted their environments. New Zealand, in particular, had protested many times about French tests. The French had repeatedly rejected protests and just carried on testing bigger and better bombs. In 1985 they exploded a blast of 150 kilotonnes, their biggest yet. There is no relief for the South Pacific islanders.

The inquiry showed that the French Secret Service was not responsible for the sinking. Many people were dissatisfied with the result.

Reporters on a French newspaper printed a story suggesting the French were guilty. They had managed to get evidence that the inquiry failed to unearth. The story was found to be true. The President eventually admitted that the French were responsible for the sinking. The French Defence Minister resigned and the two French agents were committed for trial in New Zealand.

The French continued with their tests and Greenpeace followed them in a new ship.

American tests

Bikini Island in the South Pacific was once a paradise island. In August 1978 the inhabitants left by boat for the second time. Their beautiful island had been poisoned by radiation. The 139 islanders left to an uncertain future 800 kilometres away on Kili Island.

The inhabitants of Bikini had first been forced to leave their island when the Americans decided to do nuclear tests there in the 1950s. The US had always promised that the islanders would return one day. In 1968 they were indeed returned but ten years later dangerous radiation was still found there. It was decided that the islanders must be evacuated. It did not matter that the island of Kili had no lagoons. Bikini had lagoons and was ideal for fishing. The islanders were taken on a shopping trip to a US missile base. They were given about £50 each to spend. It could be tens of years before the islanders can return. The ground, fresh water and coconuts are still poisoned by radiation.

MISSILES

Nuclear missiles can be divided into two types. They are *strategic* or *tactical*. The missiles with the longest ranges can affect the overall strategy of the war, hence they are strategic. Shorter range missiles can affect the outcome of a battle and are said to be tactical. Estimates show that the USA has about 16 000 nuclear warheads at present. The Russians have less nuclear warheads with 10 000. The USA would appear to be stronger in the air and at sea. The Russians have more land-based nuclear warheads.

Modern missiles are so accurate that it would be possible to win a nuclear war. Unfortunately for us, this could also make a nuclear war more likely. It is a pity that many of the nuclear powers are so secretive. The Russians, French, Chinese and British are very secretive about nuclear matters. It is the secrecy that feeds mistrust.

The ways a missile can track its target

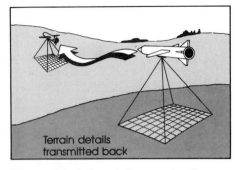

Terrain details transmitted back

The computer in the missile recognises the features of the countryside which lead to the target

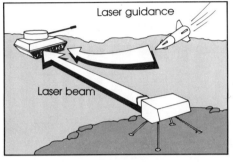

Laser guidance

Laser beam

The laser beam is pointed at the target and the missile follows the beam

Infra-red homing

Missile is attracted by the heat of the jet

The accuracy of missiles is largely due to the development of miniature computers. These can compare the geography of an area with their memory; this is called *terrain comparison*. Guidance systems may also be aided by laser beams of infra-red detection. The infra-red system is attracted to heat, such as the exhaust of an enemy aircraft.

The strategic missiles are really rockets and fit into two launch types. The *inter-continental ballistic missiles*, ICBM, are kept in missile silos and launched from earth. The silos are deep pits to disguise and protect the missiles. The other strategic missiles are submarine-launched. These are known as *submarine-launched ballistic missiles* or SLBM. Most of the missiles on submarines are aimed at cities. It is very unlikely that nuclear submarines would be amongst the early casualties in the event of a nuclear war. The knowledge that they are targeted on their cities may well deter an enemy from making the first nuclear attack.

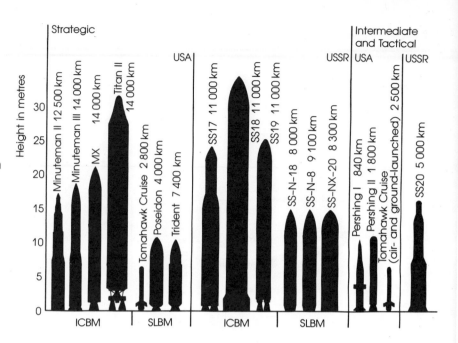

Some major American and Russian missiles and their ranges

Many nuclear warheads for both types of missile consist of a number of smaller warheads. The smaller warheads have separate guidance controls. This system is known as MIRV which stands for *manoeuvrable independently-targeted re-entry vehicle*. With the MIRV system one missile can hit many targets.

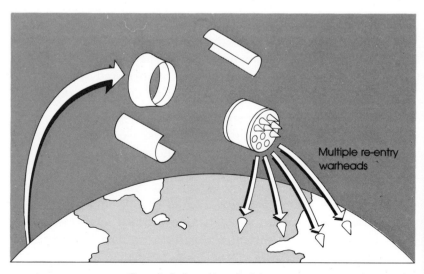

The MIRV system

The missile head breaks into many independently-targeted warheads

America relies mainly on the Minuteman III as an accurate ICBM. They are stored in silos and have a target accuracy of 200 metres. This is remarkable accuracy when you consider a journey of 14 000 kilometres. The MX missile is under development and this is even more accurate. A system of silos connected by underground roadways is planned to disguise an obvious target.

The Russians have a range of missiles known as SS and numbered 17, 18 and 19. They are all ICBMs. The SS18 is the most formidable. It will soon have an accuracy of 250 metres. Its warhead has a huge 20 megatonnes of TNT. Easily the biggest warhead on a ballistic missile.

The American submarine-launched missiles are Poseidon, Trident and Cruise (Tomahawk). The Russians have similar missiles but of greater range.

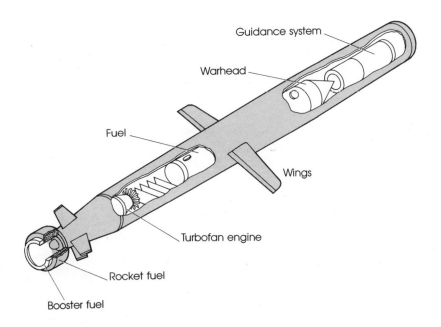

Tomahawk Cruise missile

Guidance system

Warhead

Fuel

Wings

Turbofan engine

Rocket fuel

Booster fuel

Tactical nuclear weapons are used in various missiles, land-mines, artillery shells, bombs and torpedoes. The land-based tactical systems range from twelve to a few thousand kilometres. The warheads vary in strength from ten tonnes to a megatonne of TNT.

The Russians have the SS20s as their main tactical missile. More than half of these are trained on Western Europe. Their range is thought to be about 5000 kilometres. Each missile has three independent warheads.

The Americans have Pershing and Cruise missiles for tactical use. The Cruise missile is based on the German V1 'buzz-bomb' used in World War Two. It has a very small but accurate guidance system containing a miniature computer. It can be air-, ground- or sea-launched. On ground, it can easily be launched from a mobile vehicle. This increases its chance of survival as a moving target. It also gives it a 'quick-strike' capability. It has a turbofan engine to sustain flight.

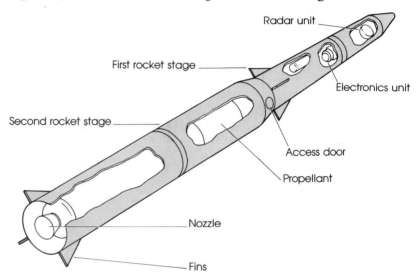

Pershing II missile

The Pershing II missile is launched vertically by a two-stage rocket motor. The fins control the flight. It is launched using the booster motor. This then burns out and falls away. The second motor then ignites thrusting the missile to the highest point of its flight. This then falls away, leaving only the war-head and guidance systems. As it nears its target, the terrain scanner checks the area against its computer.

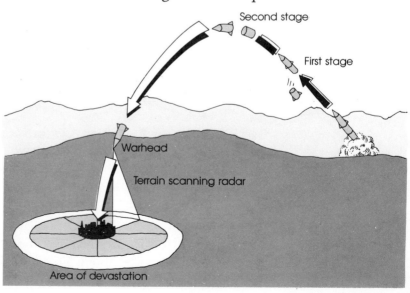

Pershing II: flight stages

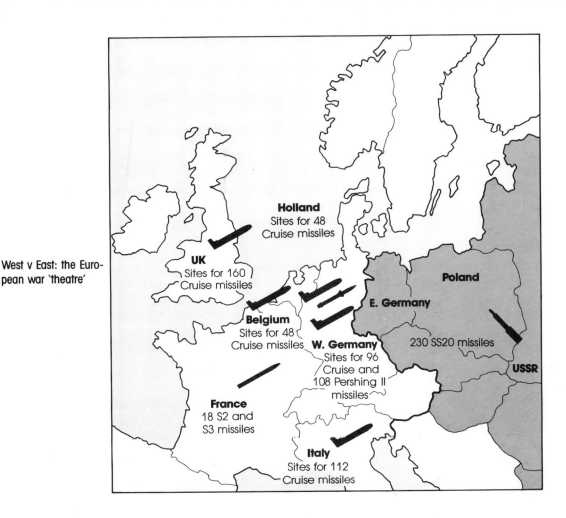

West v East: the Euro-
pean war 'theatre'

Holland
Sites for 48
Cruise missiles

UK
Sites for 160
Cruise missiles

Poland

E. Germany

Belgium
Sites for 48
Cruise missiles

W. Germany
Sites for 96
Cruise and
108 Pershing II
missiles

230 SS20 missiles

USSR

France
18 S2 and
S3 missiles

Italy
Sites for 112
Cruise missiles

There has not been a world war for forty years. Many feel
that this is because of nuclear weapons. One super power's
nuclear arsenal deters the other from attacking. This system is
officially called *mutually assured destruction*, MAD. The accuracy
of modern missiles is such that one country might be able to
knock out the enemies' missiles in their silos. If this could
happen at the first strike, a nuclear war could be won. This
would do away with MAD and would make for a world that
was even more nuclear mad, bent on destruction.

WOMEN FOR PEACE

It was a long march from Cardiff to Greenham Common near
Newbury, Berkshire. Forty women and children walked the
200 kilometres in autumn 1981. They wanted to debate the
proposed arrival of 96 Cruise missiles at the US air base at
Greenham.

A particular worry was that the Cruise missile is a 'first-strike' weapon. This suggests that they could be used to start a war. What happened to the idea that we merely wished to defend ourselves? Representatives of the Ministry of Defence did not wish to meet the women, who decided to stay and camped outside the gates of the air base.

The conditions at the camp were rather primitive. Many of the tents were simply plastic sheets suspended on poles. The toilet arrangements were poor and clean water was hard to come by. The women and children were often in damp clothing. Local residents were not keen on their new neighbours. Some women left the camp, but new ones always took their place. One baby was actually born at the camp.

Helen John, one of the founders of the camp said, 'Many of the women have never taken a strong line on anything in their lives before'. Why had they chosen this miserable life at the camp? They said they were thinking of future generations. There would not be much of a future if the Cruise missiles were used. One woman said, 'For centuries women have watched men go off to war . . . now women are leaving home for peace'. They had a most unwanted Christmas present in 1983. It was the arrival of Cruise missiles together with 1300 American servicemen to operate them. In 1985 thousands of women linked hands around the 14.5-kilometre perimeter fence as a peaceful protest.

There have been many attempts to evict the women. Some of the women have had prison sentences and still return to the camp. What have they achieved? The camp is still going in 1986 even though some of the Cruise missiles have arrived. The camp has become a focus for protests against nuclear weapons across the world.

CAMPAIGN FOR NUCLEAR DISARMAMENT

In the UK during the 1950s a strong feeling grew that nuclear weapons were evil. The horrific results of the atom bombs in Hiroshima and Nagasaki were known. A bigger and better bomb, the hydrogen bomb, was planned. Apart from the huge cost of such weapons, people felt the future of the world was at stake. Some thought that we should set a good example and simply give up all of our nuclear weapons. Such action made by one country regardless of the others is known as *unilateral nuclear disarmament*. Would other countries follow, or take advantage of our weakness? Others played much safer and suggested countries must all agree on disarmament. If all countries agree, this is known as *multilateral nuclear disarmament*.

The Campaign for Nuclear Disarmament, CND, grew in the 1950s and has always favoured unilateral disarmament. There were regular CND marches to Aldermaston, the Atomic Weapons Research Establishment. There were also rallies and 'sit-ins' in Trafalgar Square.

As the nuclear arsenals of the super powers have grown, CND seem to have made a comeback. The 1980s have seen nuclear disarmament groups blossom across Europe. Strangely little talk of disarmament comes from Russian and Chinese people. It could be that they know little of the weapons. They may not be allowed to demonstrate.

On 24 October 1981, a CND march finished at Hyde Park Corner in London. The rally which followed attracted 250 000 sympathisers. This was a sure sign of growing concern about nuclear weapons. There were punks, nuns, children and trade unionists. Poets, teachers and architects were also there, as well as members of 'Women for Life on Earth'. Before you believe those who say CND is Communist-inspired, remember that Monsignor Bruce Kent, the Vice-President of CND, is a Catholic priest. There *were* Communists there, but there were also many people with other political beliefs too.

Hugely attended nuclear disarmament rallies have also taken place elsewhere in Europe. 200 000 people attended a rally on the Hofgarten University site in West Germany in 1981. A million people met in Central Park, New York to show their distaste for nuclear weapons. This meeting was in June 1982. The 'green' environmental party in West German politics is strongly anti-nuclear. The Green Party is steadily growing in importance in Germany. In 1982, the Nobel Prize was given to two people who have campaigned for peace all their lives. Both were against nuclear weapons.

I wrote to the Secretary of State at the Ministry of Defence asking for a clear statement on why Britain has nuclear weapons. The reply was clear and explained that our weapons are to *deter* the enemy from attacking. The enemy must know that they would lose more than they would gain by an attack. This policy has been followed for 35 years and has worked. I include the full letter for you to read.

I sent a copy of the Ministry of Defence letter to Bruce Kent, the CND Vice-President, and asked for his reply. His full letter in reply is also shown. The debate will go on. Perhaps nuclear weapons are a necessary evil. Perhaps they actually prevent wars. Ideally nuclear weapons should never have been invented but that does not help our situation today.

MINISTRY OF DEFENCE
Main Building Whitehall London SW1A 2HB

7th June 1985

Dear Mr Lee

Thank you for your letter of 21 May 1985 to the Secretary of State. I have been asked to reply.

The strategy of deterrence remains – as it has for over 35 years – the cornerstone of British and NATO defence policy. To deter successfully, we must be able – and must be seen to be able – to respond to any potential aggression in such a manner that the costs we would exact would substantially exceed any gains the aggressor might hope to achieve. We, and our NATO Allies, are under no illusions about the dangers of a nuclear war between the major powers; we believe that neither side could win such a war. But this recognition on *our* part is not sufficient to prevent the outbreak of nuclear war; it is essential that the Soviet leadership understand this as well. We must make sure that the Soviet leadership, in calculating the risks of aggression, recognises that because of our retaliatory capability, there can be no circumstance in which it would benefit by beginning a war at any level or of any duration. If the Soviets recognise that our forces can and will deny them their objectives at whatever level of conflict they contemplate, and in addition that such a conflict could lead to the destruction of those political, military and economic assets that they value most highly, then deterrence is effective and the risk of war diminished. It is this outcome we seek to achieve.

I am sure that you will understand that the Secretary of State is not able to reply personally to the very large number of letters he receives on this and other issues. However I hope that this reply has been helpful.

Yours sincerely

COLIN PARNELL

Campaign for Nuclear Disarmament

22-24 Underwood Street · London N17 7JQ

14th August 1985

Dear Mr. Lee,

Thank you for your letter about deterrence which is a long word meaning that you think you can frighten people into not attacking you by what you can do to them in return. It has not much to do with peace. You cannot get peace out of terror. . . . During the last 40 years when nuclear deterrence has been supposed to bring peace possibly as many as 20 million people have died in other wars like Vietnam and Afghanistan. Many of those wars have actually been the result of superpower conflict fought out in other countries.

One thing those who support nuclear deterrence never explain is why it is necessary to have as many bombs as the other side to frighten them. Both Russians and Americans can easily destroy all each other's major cities now. If that doesn't frighten their leaders enough what will?

. . . They never explain how you stop accidents from happening. Accidents do happen and you cannot frighten them into not happening. Yet all the time, because of the speed and accuracy of new weapons we are cutting down on the time for correcting accidents. There have been many accidents with nuclear weapons and the computers connected with them. If we go on as we are, the time will come when a nuclear attack or explosion will happen by accident. That will be the end of us all.

Last of all there are people who use the word deterrence but actually mean being able to win a nuclear war. I think there can be no winners but not everyone does. For instance an American Defense Department document signed by Mr. Weinberger "urges preparations for winning an extended nuclear war against the Soviet Union and for waging war effectively from outer space".

So for all these reasons I think deterrence is a very dangerous policy. We should start getting rid of nuclear weapons rather than adding to their stockpiles. At the same time we all have to learn that old ways of thinking will no longer do. Defending the nation state is not the most important aim for any of us. Stopping the world from destroying itself is.

Good wishes,

BRUCE KENT

STAR WARS

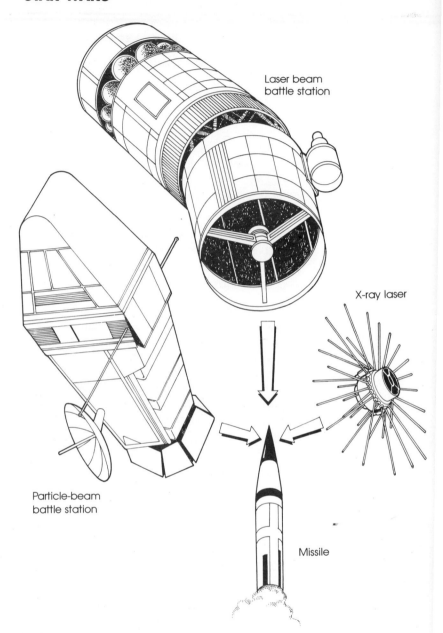

Laser beam
battle station

X-ray laser

Particle-beam
battle station

Missile

Star Wars (the Strategic Defense Initative) sounds like science fiction. The whole thing is aimed at defence against nuclear missiles. Certainly there have been no battles yet outside our atmosphere. Generals have been plotting wars in space for years. It is the new 'high ground' for warfare. It is estimated that there are about 2000 military satellites at present in space. They can spy safely at present, and some can give detail of a 20-cm object on earth. Some spy satellites are stationary above a particular spot on earth. They have the same orbit speed as the earth.

The long-range missiles have to pass through space on their way to their target. They could be destroyed as they rise out of the atmosphere or just before they re-enter it. Satellites could play a part in this destruction as a recent experiment has shown. On 21 July 1985, the very first Star Wars experiment was carried out in space. It involved the American space shuttle *Discovery*. A bluish-green laser beam was flashed towards the shuttle from a mountain in Hawaii. The space shuttle was 354 kilometres overhead. The laser beam hit a mirror the size of a dinner plate, placed in the shuttle window. The reflector bounced the beam back to Earth. The laser beam was a thin pencil of light when it left Earth. It had a 4.6 metre spread when it reached the *Discovery*. The Earth's atmosphere had spread the beam. A laser beam fired from outside the atmosphere would be much more effective. What did the experiment prove? It showed the accuracy of the laser beam to destroy missiles. The laser beam might be reflected from a satellite onto a missile being launched or in flight. If the beam were strong enough it could destroy the missile.

It is thought that Russia has 'killer satellites' which contain non-nuclear explosives. They adjust to the same orbit as an enemy spy satellite and blow it up when close. The Americans plan a missile with non-nuclear warhead to destroy satellites. The missile would be launched from an F15 jet flying in the upper atmosphere.

Various Star Wars ideas are on the drawing board in the United States. President Reagan gave the whole programme a huge boost in a speech in March 1983. He announced a programme costing 3.7 billion dollars. The American system of defence is a layered one. They have got three chances to destroy an enemy ballistic missile. They can destroy it as it rises out of the atmosphere. This would be ideal before it sends out multiple warheads in different directions (MIRV). Alternatively, they can destroy it before it re-enters the atmosphere. If both of these fail they must try an anti-ballistic missile from earth.

Three Star Wars ideas involve laser beams, particle beams or X-rays to destroy missiles.

The laser beam idea proposes a fleet of battle stations in space. They attack missiles with high-energy lasers as they enter space. There is no atmosphere to dull the laser beam. A 5-million-watt infra-red laser could be powered by a chemical reaction in space.

Battle stations could, alternatively, have particle beam generators. They would give out very high speed hydrogen atoms. These hit the missile and destroy it.

The X-ray laser would be a ring surrounded by 50 laser rods. A small atom bomb would be at the centre of the ring. The detonation of the bomb produces an intense burst of X-rays. The X-rays stimulate the laser rods and they give out a very strong X-ray pulse. The pulse would destroy the missile. The atmosphere would shield us from the X-rays. This type of laser is strongly supported by Edward Teller, inventor of the American H-bomb.

Many scientists are uncertain about Star Wars. Some feel that it just cannot be done. Certainly the apparatus for a laser beam is very bulky at present. Lasers would have to be made smaller for space. If only one super power develops space lasers, the balance of power would again be upset. This could make a nuclear war more likely.

QUESTIONS ON CHAPTER 4

In questions 1–3, supply words to fill in the blanks. Do not write on this page.

1 Modern bombs have their strengths compared to _____ the chemical _____ . A one mega_____ bomb is the same as one _____ tonnes of _____ .

2 Missiles can be _____ or _____ depending on the distance they can travel. _____ missiles are to do with the overall plan of a war. _____ missiles are to do with a particular battle. The term ICBM stands for inter-_____ _____ missile and these can travel great _____ with great _____ . Often the warhead has various _____ targeted heads within it and this is known as __ __ __ __ .

3 The smallest mass of _____ that will explode automatically is known as the _____ mass. One _____ can start the chain reaction in _____ and many atoms _____ releasing great _____ and two or three more _____ . This reaction is similar to a nuclear reactor but the reaction is un _____ .

4 Describe how the atom bomb works and say what sort of damage it can do.

5 In what ways is a hydrogen bomb similar to an atom bomb? Why is the hydrogen bomb said to be an improvement on the atom bomb?

6 Nuclear bombs give blast heat and radiation. What is special, in this respect, about the neutron bomb?

7 Explain how the neutron bomb works. What are its advantages over other bombs?

8 What is meant by the term 'broken arrow'? Describe two broken arrow accidents, one of which took place in the UK.

9 Write essays on two of the following, each time imagining that you are present:
(a) The day the atom bomb exploded.
(b) My time as a Bikini islander.
(c) The day we won the space war.

10 Describe how the Cruise missile works. Why are the Greenham women particularly worried about Cruise?

11 Give arguments for and against CND.

12 Comment on the present quantity of nuclear weapons in the world. How would you spend the money if suddenly nuclear weapons were unnecessary?

CROSSWORD ON BOMBS AND MISSILES

First, trace this grid on to a piece of paper (or photocopy this page – teacher, please see the note at the front of the book). Then fill in the answers. Do not write on this page.

Across

1 British Air Force (3)
5 Survivors were burnt and _____ (3)
7 Cruise, Trident and Pershing are all _____ missiles (8)
8 Film star from outer space (2)
9 Plan for winning the war (8)
12 Distress signal (3)
13 One missile can hit many targets with this (4)
14 These are the wars of the future (4)
16 British nuclear test site (9)
19 This big bird could suffer in the Australian nuclear tests (3)
21 A form of communal transport that would be 'knocked out' in a nuclear attack (3)
22 North Atlantic Treaty Organisation (4)
23 This could stop all electrical equipment working after the blast (3)

Down

1 After the Hiroshima bomb the city was a _____ (4)
2 A close witness to the Hiroshima bomb (6 and 6)
3 A first-strike missile (6)
4 Long distance missiles (4)
5 This group have a passionate wish to disarm (3)
6 These missiles will affect the outcome of a battle (8)
9 A series of Russian missiles (2)
10 Another name for a Cruise (Tomahawk) missile (3)
11 The polythene becomes this in a neutron bomb (3)
15 The A _____ is fission gone crazy (4)
17 Morning call (2)
18 The valley near Hiroshima _____ up when the bomb dropped (3)
20 Missiles that go _____ should also come down (2)

CHAPTER 5 NUCLEAR WAR

ARE WE PREPARED FOR A NUCLEAR ATTACK?

Some say that it is pointless preparing for defence from a nuclear attack. Nothing can be done, we must just sit back and hope that it simply does not happen. This is a defeatist attitude. Until 1968 this country had a good civil defence system involving many volunteers. Things have lapsed since but are just beginning to improve. The National Council for Civil Defence, NCCD, is a voluntary group pressing for better defence measures for our people. They already have 200 sympathetic Members of Parliament. Mrs Thatcher's Government have already said that they wish to increase the importance of civil defence. NCCD feel the Government is moving very slowly and may never move far enough.

The NCCD have many good ideas which could be presented by the Government as 'we care for you'. They feel that civil defence could cover other disasters as well as nuclear ones. We are not prepared for disasters like the chemical accidents in Bhopal, India, and Mississauga, Canada. Both of these disasters involved evacuating thousands of people. A good civil defence system would help in all hazards. Some important NCCD ideas are listed below.

- More nuclear shelters to give people confidence in the power to save lives.

- Every area should have up-to-date plans for evacuation at a time of disaster.

- There should be emergency medical stocks at key points over the country.

- Protective equipment and training for the public to cover the future threat of chemical and biological warfare.

- Far more research and training for civil defence.

- More note to be taken of the dangers of the NEP.

Nether Stowey is ready

Civil defence is a serious business, but it sometimes has a comic side. A sleepy village in Somerset is all prepared for nuclear war. A pretty fifteenth-century house in the main street of Nether Stowey will be the headquarters should a nuclear bomb be dropped. A retired Air Commodore lives at the headquarters and enjoys the fine view of a stream and the Quantock Hills. He and three others head the team of 200 volunteers. These volunteers have taken part in a course with Somerset County Council. They now know what to do in a nuclear emergency. The survival committee will tell the 1117 villagers about the effects of fall-out, loss of supplies and services, and the expected arrival of people from worse-hit areas.

The Air Commodore has his reasons for believing that Nether Stowey will survive a nuclear attack. It is 64 kilometres from Bristol and 48 kilometres from RAF Yeovilton. Both of these are likely targets but the village should survive. The Air Commodore says his transistor radio will survive the NEP. It is surrounded by kitchen foil to protect it. 'If cars are out of action, a messenger on a bicycle can reach Bridgwater in 45 minutes,' he says. 'There will be no communication problem in Nether Stowey.' But have they realised that Hinkley Point nuclear power station is just down the road?

Shelter shopping

If you believe that a nuclear war or a nuclear accident is possible, it may be time to buy a shelter. Some countries help you with the payment, others require you to have a shelter by law. In the UK you buy one if you can afford it. There is no encouragement by the Government. Very few people have shelters in the UK.

What is required in a good nuclear shelter? The shelter must be able to withstand the pressure of the air blast. It must not allow the nuclear radiation to enter. It must tolerate a burst of intense heat. If you are shopping for a shelter you must understand some terms. The *air blast overpressure* is the pressure above the usual atmospheric pressure which the shelter will withstand. If it is a 'one-atmosphere' shelter, it will retain its structure at one atmosphere above air pressure. A one-atmosphere shelter will do in most cases; it will retain its structure 3.2 kilometres from a 1-megatonne nuclear blast.

It is best to have the shelter underground to withstand the intense heat from a blast.

The *protective factor*, PF, tells you how safe you are from the radiation. A PF of 1000 means that the people in the shelter will receive one-thousandth of the radiation outside on the surface. The thicker and more dense the materials on the outside, the better the PF value.

You would be wise to choose a shelter with a high PF and a high air blast overpressure. The best shelter would be completely underground. The best material for the shelter is reinforced concrete. An expert should assemble the shelter so that full protection can be given. The shelter should have an air filter so that radiation cannot get in. The pump on the air filter can be hand-operated. It is likely that electricity would be cut off. The interior of the shelter should be comfortable. The Home Office say that you are likely to have to stay in the shelter for two weeks. Supplies of water and food must already be in the shelter.

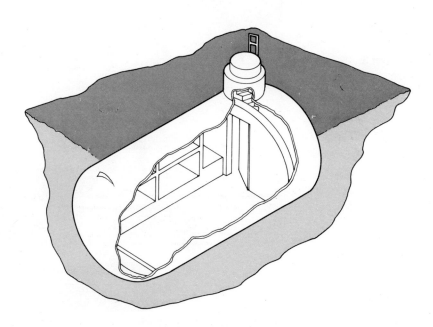

The Nesst shelter

The Nesst underground steel cylindrical shelter has an over-pressure of three atmospheres. It is made of steel 1 centimetre thick. They claim a PF of 2000 when it is surrounded by 30.5 centimetres of concrete and buried 0.9 metres below the soil.

WORLD WAR THREE

How might a third world war start if not by accident? Perhaps Russia would use tanks to move from the north to West Germany. Wave on wave of T62 battle tanks would move through NATO's front line. Russia has 20 000 such tanks and these would easily outnumber those from Western Europe and America. Anti-tank weapons and air strikes would only knock out a few enemy tanks. The call would go out for nuclear weapons.

World War 3:
Russian tanks stopped
by neutrons

The most likely nuclear weapons for use against tanks would be neutron bombs. They would be exploded in the air a few thousand metres or so above the tanks. Neutron bombs give a crippling burst of radiation which sprays out. Most of the radiation consists of neutrons. Neutrons can pass easily through the armour of the tanks and through the enemy too. Neutrons destroy living cells, particularly those of the nervous system. Most of the enemy would die over a period of weeks and few would be fit enough to drive the tanks.

What would the Russians do to counter the effects of the nuclear neutron bombs? They might counter with their own neutron bombs. They are very expensive bombs, and Russia may not have the money to develop them. They just might respond with tactical nuclear weapons. We too would then have no choice but to join them. The nuclear war might be restricted to European soil but could easily spread throughout the world. How helpless we all feel.

WHO'S AFRAID OF THE COLD AND DARK?

A medium-scale nuclear war could involve 10 000 atomic explosions. These could trigger off uncontrolled fire storms. Imagine the amount of smoke and fumes that would be generated. Some scientists are saying that this smoke could reach the upper-atmosphere some 40 kilometres above the Earth. Clouds of the smoke could drift around the world. They would cut out the Sun leaving us very cold and in the dark. This is called a *nuclear winter*. If this theory is true, it would show that no country would gain by nuclear war. The price would be severe cold and darkness for months throughout the globe. Crops would die without the Sun. Even when the nuclear winter ceased, there would be little food. What a wonderful incentive for doing away with nuclear weapons.

It must be said that many scientists take the opposite view. They suspect that the nuclear winter theory is unsound. They say that not all explosions will cause fire storms. Even if they did, they say, they would have to burn for a very long time. They also feel that little of the smoke would ever reach the outer atmosphere. Thunderstorms and rain would likely return the dust back to earth rapidly anyway, they argue. President Reagan was worried enough by the nuclear winter idea. He has ordered full studies on the subject at the cost of £40 million.

It is worth remembering that the planet Mars is so cold because it is surrounded by a layer of dust. Also when Mexico's El Chichon volcano erupted the dust sent into the air altered the weather. Some say the weather was cooler in many countries due to the volcanic dust.

CHANCES OF SURVIVAL IN THE UK

Chances of survival in the UK are small because of the geography of the country. A simple thing like a change in wind direction could drastically change the chances of survival. Populations are too concentrated in the very area where bombs would be exploded. Targets would be nuclear forces, military bases, airfields, power stations, heavy industries and institutions like the Bank of England. These tend to be surrounded by dense populations. Dr. Openshaw of Newcastle University estimates that 44 million people would die within two weeks of nuclear war. This is 80% of the population. He bases the figures on bombs totalling 219 megatonnes of TNT. This is the lowest estimate of total bombs to reach the UK in the case of a nuclear attack.

PREVENTION IS BETTER THAN CURE

Doctors today spend most of their time trying to cure their patients. Medicine in the future will surely consist of trying to prevent the illness in the first place. Many doctors feel that they will not be able to cope with the vast number of casualties in a nuclear war.

North Wales Health Authority has decided what it would do in a nuclear war. They would be dealing with 225 000 people and only have 129 doctors. The doctors would not be able to report for duty until the radiation levels dropped. Then they would be able to travel about tending the sick with little danger to themselves. The policy is that victims of radiation fall-out would be 'treated in the community'. This really means that nothing can be done. They will be left to die. They aim to have 33 casualty centres for other patients. Red Cross and St John Ambulance Brigade volunteers would have to assist the doctors.

In Cambridge in 1982 a group of doctors from all over the world met to discuss nuclear war. They were a group known as International Physicians for the Prevention of Nuclear War. Their message is that prevention is the only way. They say that any survivors of a nuclear war would be haunted until the end of their days, not only by the physical injuries but also by the suffering of the mind. Their children and grand-children, even before they are born, will be in danger, they say. The danger will be that the children will suffer inherited defects. The radiation received by their parents or grandparents will have caused these defects. There will also be an increased chance of cancer in the children. Some of the disturbing findings of the meeting are:

- There would be only one doctor per thousand seriously injured patients. Many hospitals and medical stores would be destroyed in the nuclear blast.

- Radiation reduces the natural immunity we have from disease. This means that there would be serious problems of infection and diseases would spread easily.

- Medical planning for a nuclear war is often done without involving many doctors. Doctors wish to have a say in the plans. The excuse given by the authorities is that the plans must be kept secret.

- They are worried by a nuclear winter. What will be done about the forest fires?

- Too little is said about the long term effects of a nuclear war. The biological systems in the oceans would be upset. There would be a shortage of food due to crops being ruined by radiation and the blast. The formation of vast quantities of nitrogen oxides in the atmosphere would make acid rain and attack our lungs. Many forms of cancer would develop in the long term.

The co-founders of International Physicians for the Prevention of Nuclear War were awarded a great honour on 12 October 1985. American Professor Bernard Lown and Russian Professor Yevgeny Chazov were awarded the Nobel Peace Prize. This prize gave their cause over £100 000 and gave great publicity to their work.

QUESTIONS ON CHAPTER 5

In questions 1–3, supply words to fill in the blanks. Do not write on this page.

1 The NCCD think that civil _____ should cover all _____ . Even _____ accidents like Bhopal and _____ would then be helped. There should be far more _____ in the UK, both personal and _____ ones.

2 Radiation causes burns and lowers the _____ of people to _____ . Many _____ feel that there has not been enough thought about the long _____ effects of _____ . They have formed International _____ for the _____ of Nuclear War. _____ think that _____ is better than cure.

3 When buying a shelter, its power to withstand _____ without collapsing and its power to keep out _____ , are the most important points. It is best to build it _____ and not to do it _____ .

4 What are the problems with civil defence in the UK today? How would you improve the situation?

5 What is involved in a nuclear electromagnetic pulse?

6 Describe how a nuclear winter could happen. What do the opponents of this theory say against it?

7 Write essays on two of the following, each time putting yourself into the situation:
(a) How I survived the nuclear attack.
(b) World War Three.
(c) Nuclear winter.

8 What are the chances of survival in the case of a nuclear war in the UK?

9 Give the reasons why some doctors are so worried about nuclear war.

WORDFINDER ON NUCLEAR WAR

First, trace this grid on to a piece of paper (or photocopy this page – teacher, please see the note at the front of the book). Then solve the following clues and put a ring around the answers. Answers go in any direction: across, back, up, down and diagonally. Do not write on this page.
The answer to the first question has been ringed to help you.

A	C	K	B	E	N	B	N	W	O	S	B
D	G	H	R	G	E	N	I	C	Y	Z	H
E	R	U	C	A	M	R	E	U	C	O	O
J	W	K	A	L	D	Q	H	S	A	D	P
F	I	R	E	S	H	E	L	T	E	R	A
D	N	I	W	P	S	T	O	W	E	Y	L
Y	T	W	S	R	D	I	B	I	J	L	R
F	E	Z	L	Z	R	L	S	O	K	E	O
H	R	V	O	L	A	E	A	S	G	L	T
S	E	N	W	S	Z	R	L	C	I	P	C
D	E	P	T	U	A	V	H	O	T	M	O
S	C	A	D	W	H	Q	F	P	M	N	D

1 Canadian chemical disaster here (11)
2 Prevention is better than _____ (4)
3 The Nether regions for nuclear attack (6)
4 Best buy one to survive (7)
5 Some say civil defence should cover all _____ (7)
6 An Indian chemical disaster here (6)
7 Nuclear free _____ are common in many areas of the United Kingdom (5)
8 This expert could be a great help after nuclear attack (6)
9 The likely number of weeks to be spent in a shelter (3)
10 World War _____ must never happen (5)
11 A group very keen on civil defence (4)
12 Wrap the radio in this to protect it from NEP (4)
13 Weather condition that could greatly change our chances of survival (4)
14 The nuclear _____ theory suggests a cold time (6)
15 Not a 'wet' (3)
16 Absence of light (4)
17 Barbaric, but it seems necessary (3)
18 Forests could be destroyed by this in a nuclear attack (4)

Answers to crossword on radiation and its uses

Across

3 Germs
4 Isotope
6 Beta
7 Chemistry
9 Badges
11 Curie
15 Milk
16 Aid
17 Norm
18 Radiations
20 Arthur
21 Mass

Down

1 Pitchblende
2 Atom
5 Eat
8 End
10 Gamma
12 Uranium
13 Iodines
14 UK
19 Air

Answers to wordfinder on nuclear power stations

1 Neutron
2 Fuel
3 AGR
4 PWR
5 Decommission
6 Coolant
7 Magnox
8 CEGB
9 Jet
10 Coal
11 Moderator
12 Safe
13 Sizewell
14 Fast
15 Idle
16 Venom
17 USA
18 Chain

Answers to crossword on bombs and missiles

Across

1 RAF
5 Cut
7 American
8 ET
9 Strategy
12 SOS
13 MIRV
14 Star
16 Maralinga
19 Emu
21 Bus
22 NATO
23 NEP

Down

1 Ruin
2 Father Siemes
3 Cruise
4 ICBM
5 CND
6 Tactical
9 SS
10 Tom
11 Gas
15 Bomb
17 Am
18 Lit
20 Up

Answers to wordfinder on nuclear war

1 Mississauga
2 Cure
3 Stowey
4 Shelter
5 Hazards
6 Bhopal
7 Zones
8 Doctor
9 Two
10 Three
11 NCCD
12 Foil
13 Wind
14 Winter
15 Dry
16 Dark
17 War
18 Fire

INDEX

AGR   22
Alpha radiation   2
Atom bomb   53
Atoms   3–4

Beta radiation   2
Bikini   64
Bombs   53–6
Breeder   23
Broken arrow   60–1

Cancer   6, 15, 28, 44, 58, 84
Chain reaction   20, 53
Chernobyl   28
Civil defence   79–80
CND   70–1
Coolant   22
Critical mass   53
Cruise missile   67
Curie   3

Dating   11
Decommissioning   32–3
Deterrence   72–3
Deuterium   34
Disarmament   70

Elstow   48–9

Fall-out   54
Fast reactor   23
Fission   20–1
Fusion   33–4

Gamma radiation   2
Greenham women   69–70
Greenpeace   46, 49, 63

Half-life   12–13
Health risks   15
High level wastes   42–4
Hiroshima   56–9
Hydrogen bomb   54

ICBM   65–6
Intermediate waste   41–2
Isotopes   5

JET   34

Kidney efficiency   7
King Arthur's Table   11–12

Laser beams   65, 74–6
Low level wastes   40–1

MAD   69
Magnox   22
Maralinga   62
Metal fatigue   9–10
Melt-down   26–7
MIRV   66
Missiles   64–9
Moderator   22
Mururoa   63

Nagasaki   58
Neutron bomb   55, 82
NEP   59, 79
Nuclear tests   62–4
Nuclear winter   83

Pathways   16
Pershing missile   68
Proliferation   55
PWR   22, 26, 29

Rail crash   50-1
Rainbow Warrior   63
Reactors   20–2
Reprocessing   38

Sea dumping   49
Sellafield   44–7
Shelters   80–1
Shock wave   60
Shoreham   31–2
Sizewell   29–31
SLBM   65
Star Wars   74–6
Sterilising   8

Three Mile Island   26–7
TNT   53–4
Tritium   34

Vitrification   43

Waste   39–44
World War Three   82–3

X-ray laser   76